Game Situation Training for Soccer

Themed Exercises and Small Sided Games

by Wayne Harrison

REEDSWAIN

**Library of Congress
Cataloging - in - Publication Data**

by Wayne Harrison
    Game Situation Training for Soccer
    Themed Exercises and Small Sided Games

ISBN No. 1-59164-098-9
Lib. of Congress Catalog No. 2005926724
© 2005

*Art Direction, Layout and
Proofing*
Bryan R. Beaver

Diagrams made with
easySportsGraphics
www.sports-graphics.com

Cover Photos by
Steve Griffith
Robyn McNeil

Printed by
DATA REPRODUCTIONS
Auburn, Michigan

Reedswain Publishing
562 Ridge Road
Spring City, PA 19475
800.331.5191
www.reedswain.com
info@reedswain.com

TABLE OF CONTENTS

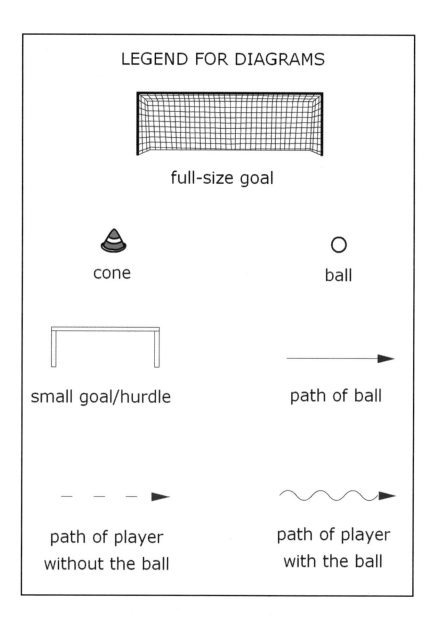

LEGEND FOR DIAGRAMS

full-size goal

cone

ball

small goal/hurdle

path of ball

path of player
without the ball

path of player
with the ball

INTRODUCTION

This is a book designed to help coaches introduce relevant themes within soccer into game orientated training situations.

The games are designed to be easily set up and executed and be a learning platform for players to perform in.

Much of the learning can involve trial and error within the game and in some ways the set up of the game can teach the theme itself to add to the coach offering input and direction.

The themes have been bracketed into the relevant chapters in the book that include possession themes, shooting themes, defending themes, heading the ball themes, target game themes, transition play themes, small sided game themes and so on.

All sizes of small sided games are covered, from a 3 v 3 format up to an 8 v 8. Various themes are presented within the 3 v 3 and 4 v 4 set ups where we are working within triangles and diamonds.

Coaches encourage the players to play at match speed in all situations so as to reproduce what actually happens in the real game situation.

Coaches can revise and develop these games to suit their own team and their own situations and may take a particular theme in another direction. This is greatly encouraged by the author because new ideas of games will result from this type of experimentation.

Examples may be; some equal number sized games in the book may need an overload to make them work initially depending on the ability of the players involved, others where an overload is used in the book may not need this and the coach can start with equal numbers based on the players ability.
Some game plans need much more attention to detail with more diagrams to show the game progressions more clearly.

Enjoy the book.

POSSESSION GAMES

40x40

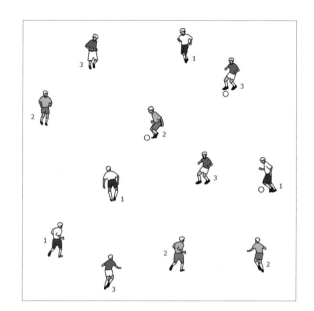

GAME OBJECTIVE: TEACHING PLAYERS TO BE AWARE OF THEIR NEXT OPTION "BEFORE" THEY RECEIVE THE BALL

1. You can have players static to begin then have them passing and moving. Player receives from the same person and passes to the same person each time. This develops great awareness of time, space and player positions. Continuous work on and off the ball.
    Awareness of: where the player you receive from is and where the player you pass to is. Because of this players begin to anticipate the pass to them and where it is coming from. Also they must look to where it is going to (where is the player they are passing to?).

2. **Coaching Points:**
    a) Creating Space
    b) Quality Passing
    c) Support positioning; early movement off the ball
    d) Players look before they receive to see own players positions, opponents players positions and space.
    e) Players are looking two moves ahead not just one.For instance as (1) is about to pass to (2), (3) should be looking to support (2) for the next pass already, looking two moves ahead before the ball leaves (1). Peripheral Vision Development results from this.

5

NON-COMPETITIVE AWARENESS NUMBERS "GAME" WITH TEAMS: PASSING IN SEQUENCE

40x40

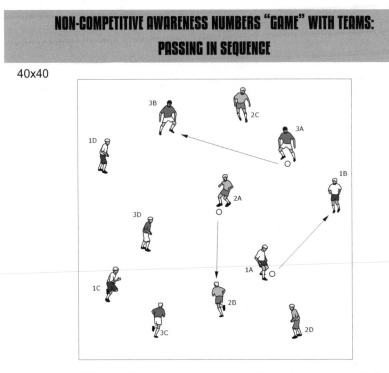

1. 3 teams. Within each numbered team each player is assigned a letter. Teams (1) and (2) work together (with two balls) and team (3) works alone (with one ball). Players must pass in sequence ie with teams (1) and (2) working together 1 passes to 2; 2 passes to 3; 3 to 4 and so on up to 8 who passes to 1 and we begin again while team (3) players pass 1 to 4. Players receive from the same person   and pass to the same person each time. This develops great awareness of time, space and player positions.Continuous work on and off the ball.

2. **Awareness of:** location of the player you receive from and the player you pass to. Because of this, players begin to anticipate the pass to them and where it is coming from. Also they must look to see where the next pass is going. We are trying to create a situation where players are looking two moves ahead, not just one. As (1) is about to pass to (2), (3) should already be looking to support (2) for the next pass

3. **Progression:** Reduce the number of touches players are allowed each time they receive a pass: 3 touch, 2 touch, then one touch if it is on to do so. This speeds up the decision making process and forces them to look earlier as to where they are passing to.

40x40

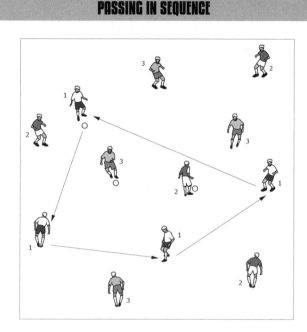

1. Now have 3 teams passing separately 1 to 4 in each team, with a ball each team. An example is the number One team. Of course the players are moving but it is easier to show it like this to get the idea across.

2. **Progression:**
   Count the number of passes each team get in a certain time frame adding a competitive element to the game. Who can get the highest number of passes made in a given time frame?

3. **Emphasize:**
   a) Movement "off" the ball to open up angles for passes between other players.
   b) Communication verbally between players to help them identify where they are; passing player can call who they are passing to, receiving player can ask for the pass.
   c) Ensure players spread out throughout the area to have them playing both long and short passes.
   d) Encourage fewer touches on the ball at each reception to move it around the field more quickly helping players develop good transitional play.

40x40

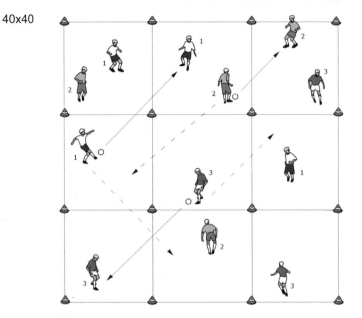

1. Conditioning the players to pass and move by setting the rule they need to move into another area once they have passed.

2. Divide the field up into sixth's and ask players to make a pass in one area then they must move to another area to receive the next pass. This can cause players to pass long or pass short and vary the range and distance of the passes and the support as they are required to move once they have made their pass.

3. Here we are using three teams of four players.

4. Here players pass and move into other zones to receive the next ball that is coming. This ensures players get the idea of passing and MOVING off the ball, not passing and then standing.

5. Can say players must pass to space so they pass into another zone next to the one the player they are passing to force them to move to the ball.

COMPETITIVE NON - DIRECTIONAL THREE TEAM AWARENESS POSSESSION GAME
(4 v 4 v 4)

40x40

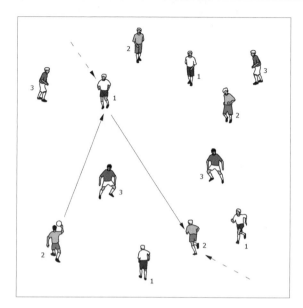

1. **Further Progression:** To make it more competitive, each team is the defending team for a certain time span. If they win the ball they give it back to the combined attacking teams. Count the number of times they win the ball. The defending team that wins the ball the most times wins the game, or alternatively the combined teams which give up the ball the fewest times win the game.

2. Attacking players individually count the number of times they give the ball away as an indication to each and every one of them how well they can maintain possession under pressure.

3. Begin with no touch restrictions, then 3 touch, then 2 touch, then 1 touch if it is on to do so.

4. **Coaching Points:**
   a) Open body stance to allow a yard or more extra space away from defenders by letting the ball run across the body into space.
   b) Looking before receiving to know in advance of the receiving pass: where the defending players are, where the space is, where teammates are free to receive a pass
   c) Movement **OFF** the ball is a priority both to receive it and after passing it.

40x40

1. Here is an interesting way to work on awareness training and passing, movement off the ball, fitness and looking for the penetrating pass. Add triangular goals to score through. The game continues after a goal is scored as the ball must be received and possession maintained by another player on the other side of the triangle to count as a goal. This ensures continuous play.

2. It is a more directional method of playing and more specific to the game in general. The defenders are **NOT** allowed inside the triangle so they must be constantly working their way around it trying to cut off the penetrating passes.

3. Team (3) defends, teams (1) and (2) work together. The combined attacking teams can attack both goals alternatively. Attacking both goals encourages "Switching the Field".

4. Ultimately reduce the game to two equal teams for the greatest challenge and reduce the number of touches progressively as they improve and are able to keep possession effectively. Reducing the number of touches inevitably increases awareness and forces players to look for options earlier and improves their decision making. This should result in better possession.

40x40

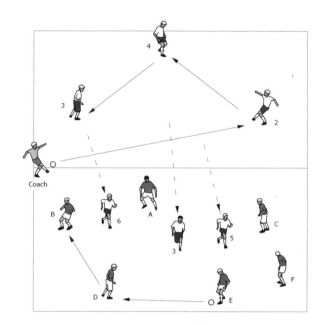

GAME OBJECTIVE: MAINTAINING POSSESSION THROUGH PASSING AND SUPPORT

1. Transition game creating 6 v 3 situations in both halves. The three defenders try to win the ball back, then they can work it back to their own half of the field. They then move back into their own half and three defenders from the other team go in to try to win it back (another 6 v 3). Whilst this is going on the three players left alone have a ball to pass to each other to keep them working, passing and moving until their teammates win the ball back, they then pass the ball to the coach who gives it to the remaining three players from the other team. Focus on what is happening on the ball, and what is happening away from the ball.

2. The three players must observe what is happening in the other half whilst passing their own ball around so that when their teammates win possession and bring it back into their own half they are ready to receive and also they see the time to play their own ball to the coach.

40x40

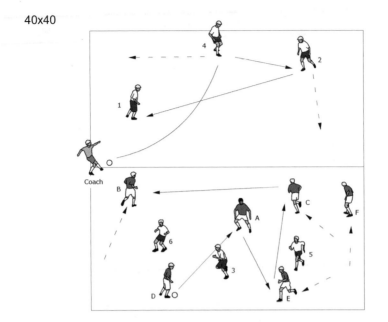

1. Here the letters team maintain possession in a 6 v 3 overload. Players are moving effectively off the ball to help each other.

2. **Coaching Points for Attacking:**
   a) Creating Space to receive or draw opponents away from space for team-mates
   b) Quality Passing (weight, accuracy, timing, short and long)
   c) Support Positions (angle, distance, communication)
   d) Switching Play (moving the ball around using the overload advantage)
   e) Maintaining possession

3. **Progression:**
   a) If they are maintaining possession too easily limit the number of touches each player has, make the game 3 or 2 touch with a goal awarded for every successful 1 touch pass (reward quick possession play)
   b) If they are not maintaining possession easily then limit the defenders to 2 rather than 3 and have a 6 v 2 in each area so the focus is on passing, possession and support not effective defending.

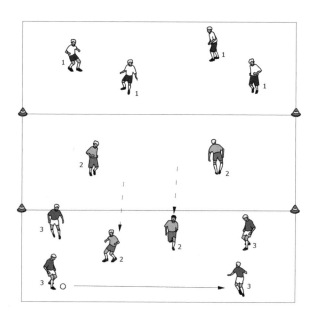

GAME OBJECTIVE: MAINTAINING POSSESSION UNDER PRESSURE AND SWITCHING THE PLAY

1. Same idea as the last slide but with a different set up. Three zones with three teams of four players. This is a possession session creating a 4 v 2 situation at each end zone. The team in possession have to make so many passes (3 for example) then pass through or over the middle team to the far team.

2. If the two defenders win it they take it back to the middle, the team who lost it go in the middle to try to win it back.

3. It is then a 4 v 4 in the middle. When they win the ball back they must get it back into their own zone and it goes to a 4 v 2 again.

4. Three consecutive passes and they pass it over or through the middle to the other team.

45x30

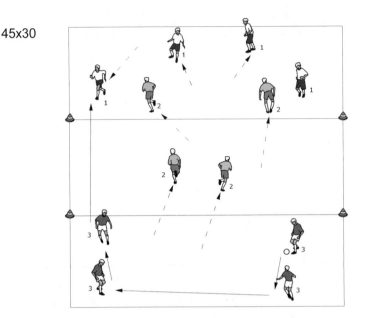

1. **Example 1:** If the attacking team make 3 passes they have to pass the ball long into the other team and through the 2 defenders in the middle either driven on the ground or chipped through the air.

2. Once the ball is in the other side the first two defenders drop back into the middle the other two defenders then attack and try to win the ball in the other third. Defenders (C) and (D) recover back into the middle, defenders (A) and (B) move into the other third and pressure the ball. Numbers team must spread out to try to keep possession and use the 4 v 2 advantage.

3. This game is a continuous sequence of passing and then switching the play.

4. **Coaching Points for Attackers:**
   a) Creating Space (using all the available space in a tight area)
   b) Quality Short and Quick Passing
   c) Quality long driven or chipped passing
   d) Support positions (movement off the ball)
   e) Maintaining possession of the ball
   f) Switching the point of attack

45x30

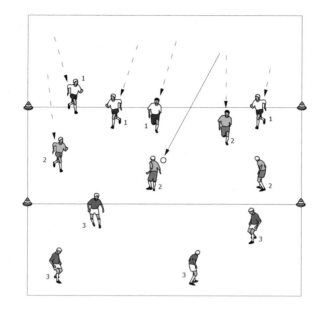

1. **Example 2:** The middle zone defending team win the ball and get it back to the middle.

2. The numbers team must try to win it back and get it back to their own zone where it becomes a 4 v 2 again. In the middle it is a 4 v 4.

3. Rotate the teams so each team has a spell in the middle zone as the defending team.

4. If players have difficulty making it work with a 4 v 2 and the ball is always being lost and taken into the middle then use a 4 v 1 so it is easy to get the sequence going.

5. If too easy with a 4 v 2 then go to a 4 v 3 to give them a bigger challenge. The coach needs to observe the session and adjust it accordingly to ensure the challenges are competitive enough.

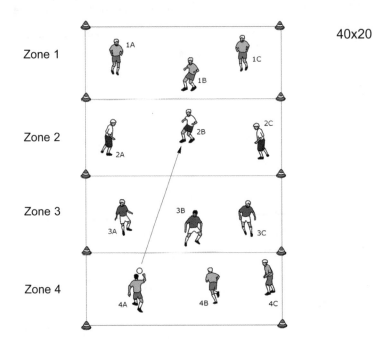

40x20

GAME OBJECTIVE: QUALITY PASSING IN LIMITED SPACE

1. Four zones with three players in each zone. Players must stay in their own zones. Passing and support game where each team gets a goal / point by passing the ball over 2 grids. Making interceptions is the way to win the ball.

2. They must pass through another grid where the players are positioning to try to intercept the pass. To make this work the players who are receiving need to keep moving to create an angle for the passer to be able to see them with regard to the players in front of them.

3. Keep score and make it competitive, each team counting the number of goals they score over a given time period. Rotate the teams so they are passing to different players and defending against different players.

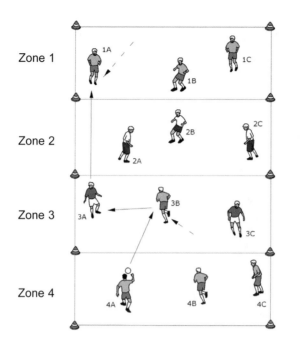

Zone 1

Zone 2

Zone 3

Zone 4

40x20

1. **Coaching Points For Attacking:**
   a) Creating Space: Movement to create an angle to receive a pass
   b) Quality of Pass (weight, accuracy and timing)
   c) Quality first touch to receive and keep possession

2. Here (D) in zone 3 intercepts the pass from zone 4 to zone 2 and now this team must get the ball to the team in zone 1. Player (D) passes to player (B), and player (4) moves to open up the passing channel to receive the pass.

3. **Progression:**
   a) Increase the difficulty by making it a 2 touch game so control, passing and decision making have to be faster
   b) Limit the number of passes in each zone, for example they must pass it to the other zone within 4 passes so awareness and decision making need to be quicker.

4. Change the focus and work on defending players to coach how to make interceptions and close down space as a unit (see defending games).

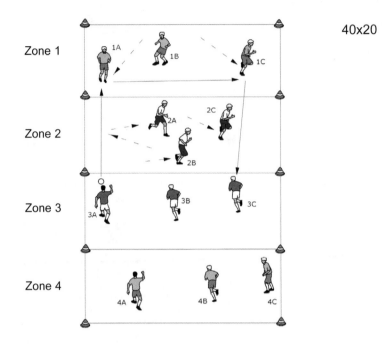

40x20

Zone 1

Zone 2

Zone 3

Zone 4

1. The secret for the attacking team is top spread out as much as they can so the defenders have more space to cover.

2. More space to cover means more space to pass through and moving the ball quickly with few touches means the defenders have to move quickly to stop the forward passes.

3. Here (4) passes to (3). The defending team in zone 2 have to adjust across to stop (2) from passing to the numbered team in zone 3.

4. If the defenders do not move as a unit then spaces open up between them and the team in possession can use these passing lanes to transfer the ball.

5. The defender cannot quite get there to stop the pass and it goes without interception to (C) in zone 3.

6. This helps speed up passing and moving on and off the ball.

40x40

GAME OBJECTIVE: IMPROVING PASSING AND DRIBBLING

1. It is a 6 v 4 overload game. 6 attack and 4 defend the circle. No one is allowed inside the circle except an attacking player on the team of 6 dribbling the ball and in possession. Attacking team keep possession and score by a player dribbling the ball into the circle. Trying to get a player free to dribble.

2. Attacking team can also score a goal by making 5 consecutive passes. This prevents the defending team just guarding the circle and not trying to make any tackles and win the ball. Defending team score by winning possession and dribbling the ball outside the square.

3. **Coaching Points for Attackers:**
    a) Creating Space (spreading out, using all the space available)
    b) Individual dribbling skills
    c) Quality quick Passing
    d) Support: Movement off the ball to find space to receive or create space for other team mates
    e) Maintaining Possession

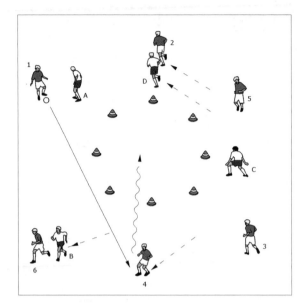

1. **Coaching Points for Defenders:**
   a) Quick individual player pressure
   b) Working in pairs to force mistakes or win the ball quickly
   c) Collective team Defending where possible (numbers around the ball)
      boxing players in.

2. (4) moves into space to open up the angle for a pass from (1). (4) can now dribble into the scoring circle in the middle.

3. Likewise (6) and (2) move and open up the angle for a pass but defenders (D) and (B) anticipate this and track the runs by (2) and (6).

4. What (6)'s movement does though is open up a passing lane for (4) to receive, so (6)'s movement was not only to receive a pass themselves if this player got free, but also to help a pass to (4).

5. This type of movement from an attacking point of view is so important in soccer because players need to learn how to make movements for team-mates in an unselfish way.

40x40

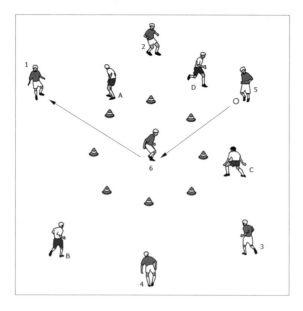

1. **Progressions:**
   a) Have an attacking player stationed in the middle all the time and use this player as a link player, scoring a point every time a pass is made to them by the attacking team.
   b) To score a player has to arrive in the circle as the ball arrives. If they don't get the ball they move out again for someone else to fill the space and receive the pass the next time.
   c) Change it to a keeper in the circle to give the keeper some handling work. Every time the keeper catches the ball it is a goal.

2. Defending team still scores by running the ball outside the square.

3. Make it an equal numbers game so both teams can attack and can use the keeper to pass to or have an outfield player in the middle to pass to for both teams.

4. Condition the game to one and two touch (one touch only when it is on to do so). Hence timing of the pass and timing of the run in a) and b) are especially important when the player only has one or two touches.

15x15

GAME OBJECTIVE: FOCUS ON IMPROVING MOVEMENT "OFF" THE BALL

1. Here is an interesting way to work on passing, movement off the ball, fitness and looking for the penetrating pass. Start with a 15 x 15 yard grid and have a 4 yard equilateral triangle in the middle made up of cones. There are 5 players in the activity with one being a defender and the other four being on offense. The 4 players try to maintain possession while also looking to score goals by playing the ball through the triangle to their teammates. The defender is NOT allowed inside the triangle so he or she must be constantly working their way around the triangle trying to cut of the penetrating passes. See the diagram above for the set up.

2. Note the required movement off the ball by the offensive players. On every pass they are moving in order to get into a better position to either make a penetrating pass or to receive one (as opposed to the norm in possession games when players wait till they receive a ball before thinking what to do next, in this game the players have to be thinking ahead of the passes because it's not good enough to just play the ball through the triangle, a teammate has to be there and receive the ball for it to count.

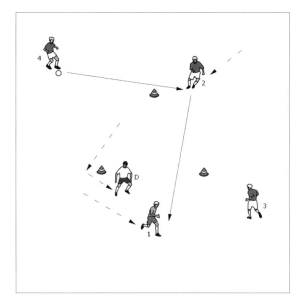

3. Play this game for a 5 minute period with each player having a one minute turn on defense. It gets the players working hard, thinking and competing while having fun trying to beat their teammates. The player who gives up the fewest number of goals on defense wins. There is a tendency in this game for the offensive players to get too close to the triangle, which takes away the passing angles (just like in a regular game where they come to close to the middle). This is easy to correct and is a good learning opportunity for the players. Above (D) stops the immediate pass from (4) to (3) through the triangle so (4) passes to (2) and (1) makes a run off the ball to receive the next pass through the triangle and a goal is scored. (D) tries to get back and around to prevent this.

4. **Coaching Points:**
   a) Creating Space for yourself or for a team mate by movement off the ball
   b) Quality of Passing (weight, accuracy and timing)
   c) Quality of Control and first touch
   d) Effective maintenance of possession

5. **Progression:** Change to 4 v 2, or 2 v 2 v 2. Keep the overload initially until players get good at this before you move on. Experiment with numbers increasing the difficulty of the session as you go.

30x30

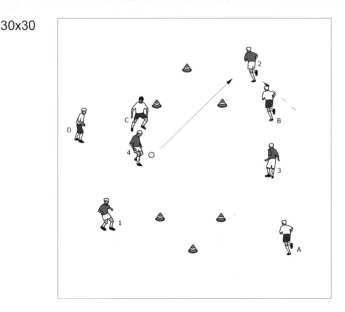

1. **Coaching Points:**
   a) Creating Space with movement off the ball
   b) Quality Passing
   c) Support positions of team mates
   d) Maintain Possession

2. Increase the area to 30 x 30 and have a 3 v 3 or 4 v 4 game (as above) and two triangular goals. (Numbers team attack one goal and letters team attack the other.

3. **Progression:**
   Each team can score through both goals but it must be a pass and receive from one player to another through the middle of the triangle. This brings more switching the point of attack into the game.

4. Condition it where once you score through one you need to try to score through the other. You can 't go back to the goal you score previously until possession has changed and you have regained possession again. Players can also score a goal by keeping possession and making 5 consecutive passes without an interception.

30x30

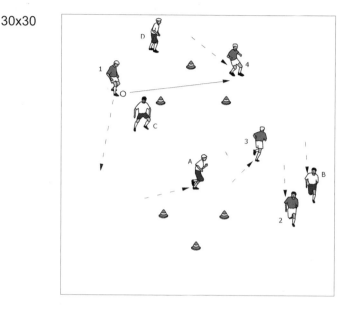

1. Here (4) receives the pass into space from (1) after (2) has created the space by a run away from it.

2. Looking ahead, (3) makes a run into space to now help (4) and gets away from marker (A).

3. (1) makes a blind side run behind (C) to help (3) if he or she should receive the next pass, either as a pure pass or a pass through the goal to score.

4. Lots of movement off the ball by the players to either get it themselves or to help another player receive the pass.

5. I have made it look easier by not having defenders always track the runs but I do this to help emphasize how the movements off the ball can work.

6. Progress to using three then four goals.

40x40

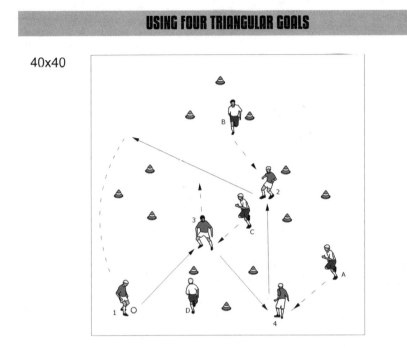

1. Using four goals now and increasing the area to a 40 x 40. The numbers team attack goals one and two, letters team attack goals three and four.

2. Above (D) blocks the straight pass so (3) makes an angle for a pass off (1); receives it and scores a goal passing through the triangle to (4).

3. (4) sees (2) in position for the next pass as the ball is traveling and plays this player a one touch pass into space.

4. (1) is already on a run off the ball to attack the other goal and give (2) a new passing option. (3) also is on the move after passing to join in the next build up.

Players often get into the habit of taking the ball back to where they are facing because of a closed stance and where the ball has just come from, these sessions are to help players get the idea of opening up their body stance to be able to switch the play in another or the opposite direction and thus get a better appreciation of the use of whole field of play.

40x40

GAME OBJECTIVE: TEACHING SWITCHING
THE POINT OF ATTACK

1. Passing and moving with two teams, one ball each then two balls each, more opportunity to switch the play, greater need to be aware of everyone's positions.

2. **Progression:** Passing and moving with two teams & inside goals to play through. Count the number of passes through the goals in a certain time (can't go back through the same goal twice). Make it competitive, start with an 8 v 4 overload.

3. Equal it up and count the number of goals scored by each team so they have a goal to aim for (first team to score 10 goals). Observe the moments when players can switch the play, do they take the opportunity?

1. We first have all the players moving freely passing and moving with in their own team. Divide the group into two teams. Begin with one ball being passed around each team and as they become proficient introduce another ball. Here we have two balls per team.

40x40

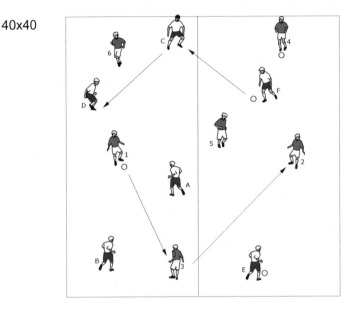

2. Often in games players have the opportunity to switch the direction that the ball is traveling but choose to take it back to where it came from and often this is back into where the opponents are strong, instead of opening their stance up and changing the field to where the opponents may be weak and your team is stronger. It is like the players are wearing blinkers and can't see around them.

3. These sessions are designed to help the players develop the capacity to look around and identify the moment they can switch the field. The presentation is based on a field set up where you can develop the session in different ways with built in progressions and as little need to change the basic set-up as possible.

4. To begin have the teams play throughout both grids to spread the play out and get the players comfortable and composed. As they improve you can change it to playing in one grid only so there is less room to work in and things happen more quickly. This is a test of their Awareness.

40x40

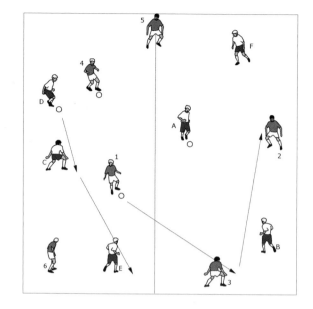

5. Introduce the concept of switching the direction of play. The receiving player lets the ball run across his body to change the direction of play. The weight of the pass is important here.They can also move the ball off at another angle to change the direction of play. One method is without a touch on the ball, the other is with a touch. The player receiving the ball should drop his shoulder one way towards the ball and check the other way with the ball to fool the defender. This is to counteract the tendency to take the ball back to where it came from due to a closed body position, which restricts the player's options. Like a horse with blinders on!!! Players must recognize where to change direction and what their options are before they receive the ball. The opposing players play passive defense, filling the same spaces.

6. **COACHING POINTS IN SWITCHING PLAY**
   a) Look before you receive – where are team mates? Opponents?
   b) Open body stance – side on to where the ball is coming from.
   c) Check towards the ball –Dummy to fool the defender in a game situation.
   d) If time and space are available, let the ball run across the body – allowing you to switch play without touching the ball. If the space is covered, move the ball in another direction with a good first touch.
   e) Pace of the pass – must be such that the player can let it run across his body and maintain possession of it.
   f) Change direction – switch from one side to the other.

40x40

1. The goals are spread out and act as a reference to help the players spread out, switch play, pass and support each other. They must make their passes through the goal. This condition forces the players to find a goal (and space) to pass and to receive through. Once they receive the ball they must then find someone else to pass to.The support players spread out to receive by moving into space (where the other goals are). In the example: (6) passes to (3) who arrives as the ball arrives at the goal. Encourage (3) to look behind or to the side (before he receives the ball) to see if there is space to move into. Here (3) can check towards the ball, let it run across his body and then move away in the direction the ball is going.

2. Two teams working in the same area means congestion, so decisions have to be made quickly on where, when and how to pass and receive. Move into an overload situation so there is opposition to increase the pressure on the players. Have an 8 v 4 in the above workout, still using the goals as points of reference for support positions. Count the number of passes made through the goals. Develop – score a goal by dribbling through the goal also.

3. **GAME:** Equal sides and make it competitive, counting passes through the goals as a goal and the first team to ten goals will be the winner.

40x40

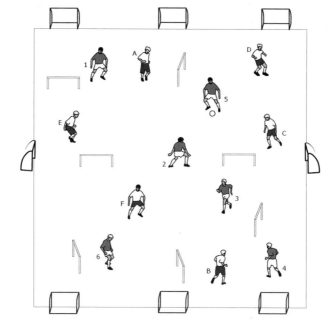

1. **Competitive Game One:** an overload situation (8 v 4) with two teams competing against each other, using only the inside goals to score a point.

2. **Competitive Game Two:** Now equal numbers (6 v 6), using only the inside goals to score a point.

3. **Competitive Game Three:** the outside three goal game with one point for a goal in the central outside goal and two for goals in the wide outside goals (because we are focusing on switching and spreading the play). Leave the two wide goals inside the grid, when players pass or dribble through them they get a point.

4. **Competitive Game Four:** A switching game using the four outside central goals on the four sides of the grid. Teams score in opposite goals, two goals to attack which are opposite each other. All the sessions are designed to help players learn how to switch the play and change the field. Using different games like these keeps the players focused and interested because of the different challenges they present.

CIRCLE
DIAMETER
APPROX.
25 YDS

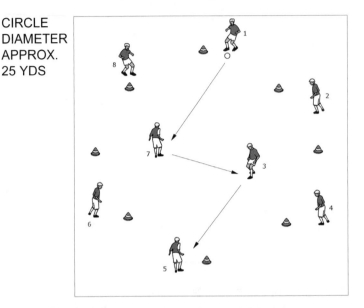

GAME OBJECTIVE: MAINTAINING POSSESSION IN
VARIOUS COMBINATIONS OF PLAYERS WITH OVERLOADS

1. **Introduction:** Two players in the middle receiving and passing. As the ball travels to (7) he has already looked to see where (3) is. (3) is already moving to a support position to be ready for (7) and at the same time is viewing the field to see who is available to receive a pass on the outside. As the ball travels to (3), ask him to call the name of the player he intends to pass to, before the ball arrives. (3) needs to look at (7), look to see who is free, then look back to see the ball as it is coming. (7) moves to an angled support position to receive the pass from (1). (3) makes an angle off (7) to receive the ball, then passes to (5).

2. **Coaching Points:**
    a) Body shape when receiving;
    b) Quality of pass (weight, timing and accuracy)
    c) Support angles
    d) Good first touch.

3. **Progression:**
    a) Three players working together in the middle
    b) Two pairs working together in the middle.

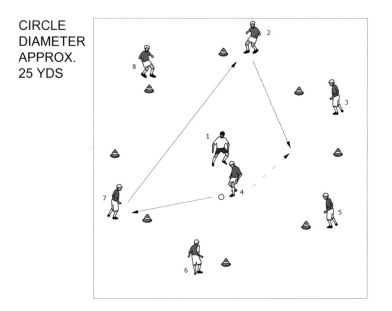

CIRCLE DIAMETER APPROX. 25 YDS

1. **1 v 1's** – Possession play (keep ball) in the middle, outside players two touch but must pass quickly to keep the pressure on inside the circle. High intensity work. Rotate players. Inside players have as many touches as they like, practicing dribbling skills in 1 v 1 situations, passing and movement off the ball, working combinations with teammates. Inside players can't tackle outside players but can intercept passes from them. Outside players move to improve support angles. Passing to both space and feet. This is a 7 v 1 in favor of the player in possession.

2. **Coaching Points :**
   a) Quality of passing (accuracy, timing and weight).
   b) Angles and distances of support.
   c) Movement "off" the ball.
   d) Communication.

3. Outside players identify who they will pass to as the ball is coming. Call a player's name to pass to "before" the pass so the inside player in posses-sion knows which player to work off next. As the ball is coming to (7), player (2) calls and asks for the next pass to make (7) aware that he is open and available. Here (4) passes to (7), who, as the ball is traveling calls out (2)'s name. This is a cue for (4) to then change position to receive the next pass from (2) early and in space. One or two touch play on the outside will mean quick passing and will help (4) get possession again early and in space away from defender (1), who hopefully has been left flat footed.

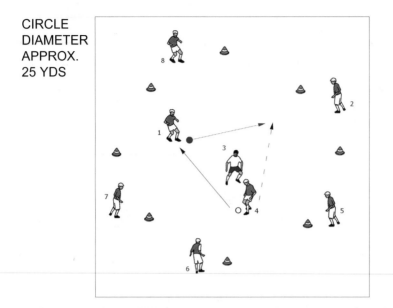

CIRCLE
DIAMETER
APPROX.
25 YDS

1. **2 v 1:** - Here we have an overload of a 2 v 1 in the middle. (1) and (4) must keep the ball away from (3) using the outside players as support.

2. If (3) wins the ball he uses the outside players to try to keep possession.

3. **Progression:** If an inside player gives the ball away, that player then becomes the defender against the other two players.

4. Players (1) and (4) must make it as difficult as possible for defender (3) to win the ball. If it becomes too easy using the outside players then limit them to one touch each and have the two inside players limited to two touch, then one touch, so the challenge becomes greater.

5. Defender (3) closes (4) down. (4) passes to (1) and moves off the ball to receive the give and go to escape the defender's attention.

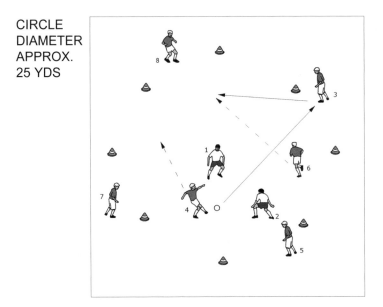

CIRCLE
DIAMETER
APPROX.
25 YDS

1. **2 v 2's** - (1) and (2) against (4) and (6). Build to 3 v 2 and so on depending on the numbers of players. Use outside players as support players for both teams.

2. Inside players can have free play, then progress to three, then two touch to improve speed of decision making. Outside players start with two touch, then move to one touch play.

3. This is technically a 6 v 2 in favor of the team in possession.

4. Keep rotating players to allow them to work with different partners. This is physical work, but players get a break on the outside to recover, ensuring quality work inside the circle.

5. Use the outside players – an example would be as above where (6) has gotten into the same passing lane as (3). (6) shapes up to receive a pass but lets it run across the body through to (3) and then makes a movement to support the next pass from (3).

6. **Progression** - As the players improve, condition the game so that there can be only three, then two passes between outside players, then the ball must be passed to an inside player. The two inside players must link up with a pass before the ball goes to an outside player again.

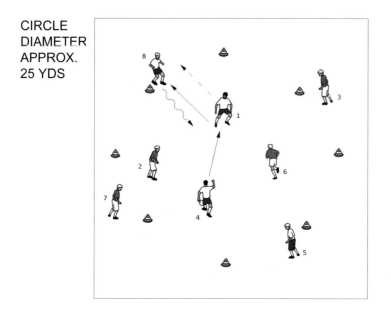

CIRCLE
DIAMETER
APPROX.
25 YDS

1. **2 v 2 in the middle,** players can only pass to their teammates on the outside to keep possession. This provides half the number of options as before.

2. **Progression:** The outside player who receives the pass from the inside player now keeps possession and goes into the middle and switches with the inside player who initially passed the ball outside.

3. The outside player coming into the circle with the ball can run it in and keep possession or pass it to his teammate one touch.

4. Constant changing of positions here means players are always on the move, both on and off the ball.

5. This is a great session for working on movement off the ball for players to support each other in tight spaces as well as developing technical skills on the ball in tight spaces.

6. Introduce a free player who works with both teams when in possession to develop the practice into a 3 v 2.

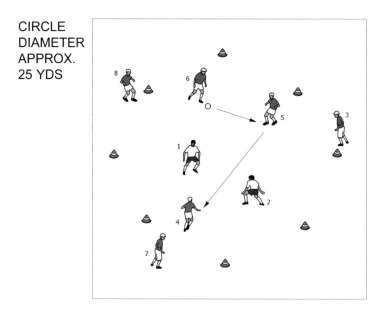

1. **3 v 2:** - Now we have an overload situation as in the 2 v 1 previously. You can bring in this set up before the 2 v 2 if you desire as it is easier to gain success with it than in the 2 v 2 and equal numbers. This is technically a 6 v 3 for the team in possession. Try to split the two defenders with a pass between them as above.

2. To make it a bigger challenge for the players, condition the number of touches they have in the circle to three, then two, then one, if it is on to do so. Try to split the defenders with a pass between them.

3. If the defenders win the ball they are outnumbered, so allow them to be free with no restriction on touches and encourage them to keep the ball using the outside players.This is their reward for winning back the ball.

4. The variations on this set up are numerous and it just takes a little imagination to develop new ideas.

5. Progress from 1 v 1, 3 v 1, 2 v 1, 2 v 2, 4 v 2, 3 v 2, 3 v 3 and so on depending on the number of players you have to work with.The area can change as you increase the number of players in the middle.

6. Use the session to improve support play or improve defensive play (when the players are outnumbered for example).

SHOOTING AND FINISHING GAMES

60x30

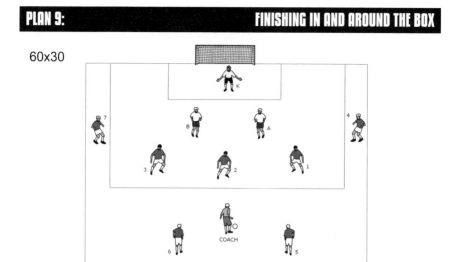

GAME OBJECTIVE: FINISHING IN AND AROUND THE BOX

1. **3 v 2 with support players** involving Receiving,Turning, Dribbling and Shooting. First priority of the striker is "Can I shoot ?" Composure in the box is the key factor, defenders don't want to concede a penalty so strikers have more time than they realize.

2. No conditions to start, support players stay outside the box. When defenders win the ball they play to the coach or clear to outside players. Strikers try to receive the ball at an angle, half turned and facing the goal so they can get a quick one touch shot in. Outside players pass a ball around between them to keep active and when the play is finished inside the box whoever is on the second ball passes it in to restart. Focus on quick shots, rebounds, combination work, 1 – 2's, quick movement to create space, support play.

3. **Coaching Points in Shooting:**
   a) Positive Attitude to shoot, quick shooting.
   b) Receive on the Half Turn if possible (create space for yourself), take chances
   c) Accuracy and Power (accuracy first). Be composed
   d) Shooting High or Low (low is best because it is more difficult for the keeper)
   e) Selection of Shot (driven, chip, side foot, swerve etc). You can use defenders to shoot around for placement. Check keeper's position.
   f) Near Post or Far Post (depends on keeper's position). Also keep in mind that if you shoot and miss at the near post the ball is out of play, if the shot is at the far post and it misses, the keeper may palm it to a striker following up, who may intercept it and score, (or it may hit a defender and go in him)
   g) Rebounds (follow all shots in)

41

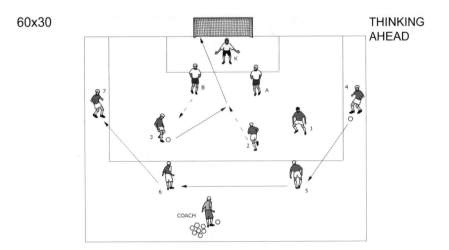

1. The shot has been taken and a goal scored, next ball is ready to pass into the box to begin the next play with (7). As soon as the first play is over the second play begins. Outside players pass a ball around to keep active.

2. Using two balls helps the players' observation, concentration and awareness. Players inside the box need to be aware that only 3 of 4 outside players are available at one time to support. Also, once the play is over they must be ready for the next one and be able to see quickly where the next ball is coming from.

3. Outside players must recognize when they need to support an inside player when the outside ball is played to them, and when it needs to be played in for the next play. Lots of decisions to be made, all leading to quick thinking and observation away from the ball as well as on the ball.

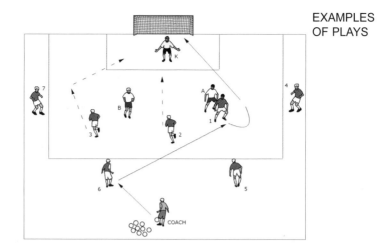

1. Examples can be a pass to (1) who beats (A) and shoots, (2) and (3) follow
   in for rebounds. (1) opens his body stance and comes off the shoulder of
   (A) to create space and an angle to receive the pass. He can shoot first
   time using the momentum of the pass or make a good first touch past (A)
   and take the shot in two touches. First touch by (1) may be back across (A)
   coming inside for the shot or a one touch finish using (A)'s position as a
   guide to bend the shot around. Strikers can use support players in link up
   play if they receive but can't turn.

2. **Progression 1:** – Condition the strikers to three touches, then two touches
   then one touch, but only if it is on to do so. Support players can change
   from two to one touch as they won't have much time on the ball in a game.
   This ensures that both strikers and support players are thinking quickly and
   ahead of the game and trying to recognize situations early.

3. Have wide players crossing the ball when they get it so players inside take
   up a position to receive from the cross. Central midfielders pass or shoot.

POSSIBLE
PASSING
OPTIONS

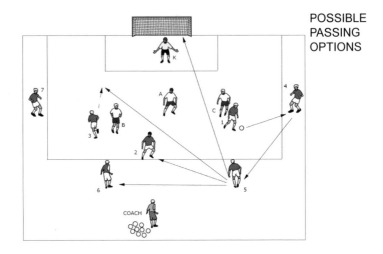

1. **Progression 2:** – When support players receive the ball, they can pass to other support players to change the direction of the attack, or shoot directly at goal with the strikers working their positions for possible rebounds.

2. As you gain success in a 3 v 2 situation, bring another defender in and play 3 v 3. Rotate players regularly to ensure quality as this session can be tiring. Introduce offside, this helps defenders and forces strikers to time their runs and take up support positions (You can work on your defenders to improve them in this session).

3. **Progression 3:** - 3 v 3 but either team can score if they get possession. For example, only attacking players are available at your session and you want them all to work on finishing (so no offside). Server calls out the team name who they'll pass to. The team adjusts positions to receive, while the other team adjusts to stop them and regain possession.

4. **Progression 4:** – Support players have a ball each and are numbered. When the coach calls a number of a server, players react accordingly. Thinking processes are: remembering where the ball is coming from and what to do when your team has the ball or when the opposition is in possession; quick decision making.

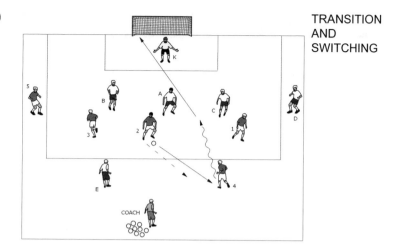

1. **3 v 2, 2 v 2, 3 v 3**, vary depending on success. Vary the number of touches on the ball. Here a 3 v 3 game but both teams have the chance to score a goal. The coach serves the ball in to each team alternately so they know if they have to create space or mark up. They can use the outside players as support but only their own teammates. Both teams can attack and both teams can defend, hence constant transitions from defense to attack and attack to defense. The 3 moments in the game now come into play; when we have the ball, when they have it and when the ball changes hands.

2. **Progression 5:** – Outside players can shoot for themselves and develop the idea of switching positions from outside to inside and vise versa, where, when the pass is made e.g. from (2) to (4), the players switch positions, one going out and the other coming into play to link up with the other inside players. (4) may come into a good position to shoot at goal. This is good because the switching movement happens in a game but it also keeps everyone involved.

3. Bring in outside players to make 4 v 4 or 5 v 5 inside the box. This is intensive work, good for seeing who can make quick decisions. Position players inside the box, two strikers centrally and two players wide and supporting midfielder inside the edge of the box centrally for lay offs so they are working from a shape.

40x30

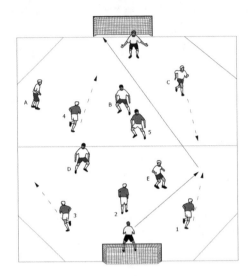

GAME OBJECTIVE: IMPROVING LONG RANGE SHOOTING

1. **Long Range Power Shooting Practice:** Encourage players to shoot whenever possible.They can only shoot from their own half of the field. The two forwards can work for rebounds.They can also be used to set up shots for support players.

2. **Coaching Points:**
   a) **Spread Out** as a team to create space to receive and shoot.
   b) **Decision** - Pass the ball until a player is in a good position to shoot
   c) **Technique** – A good first touch to set the shot up (or first time shot).
   d) **Accuracy and Power** (in this order) and **Shot Selection** (driven , swerved etc).
   e) **High / Low, Near / Far Post Shots**. (low far post is best, depending on keeper's position).
   f) **Rebounds** – They can come off the keeper, a defender or the goal. Be alert and get into position.

40x30

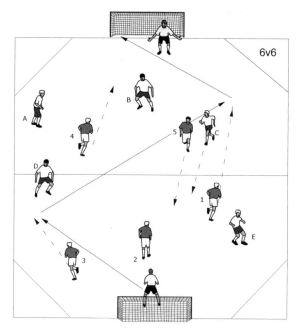

3v2 or 4v1

1. You are looking for the players' attitude to shoot, Ability to hit the target, correct selection and positioning of the shot, and anticipation positions for rebounds.

2. **Progression:** the players can move between the two halves of the field but must maintain a balance of (in the case above) three in the defending half and two in the attacking half.

3. In the example, (3) can't shoot because (D) is blocking the shot and the forward pass to (4). (5) comes short and takes defender (C) away from the space behind, (1) moves into that space and (3) passes to (1) in an attacking position to shoot at goal. Striker (4) follows in for potential rebounds.

60x40

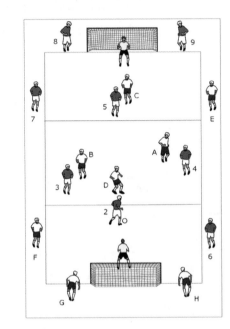

GAME OBJECTIVE: IMPROVE PASSING AND FINISHING

1. Eighteen players. A 4 v 4 game with side players to support and goal line players for 1-2's to set up shooting chances. You can vary the number of players playing in the game.

2. No offside to begin. Players on the outside need to keep on their toes. Game lasts until players begin to fatigue. Rotate outside players in, inside players out.

3. **Progressions:** – Introduce offside from the thirds.
   a) Outside players 1 or 2 touch restriction on the ball.
   b) Inside players 2 touch restriction on the ball.
   c) Player passes to an outside player and switches. This gets the players thinking, especially when the player coming in has only 1 touch and so must immediately find a player.
   d) Occasionally bring in all the players for a 9 v 9 with the keepers. This tests how they play in a restricted space with more players to deal with.
   e) Reduce the size of the area to 40 x 20, and go 4 v 4. This gets more shots on goal.

60x40

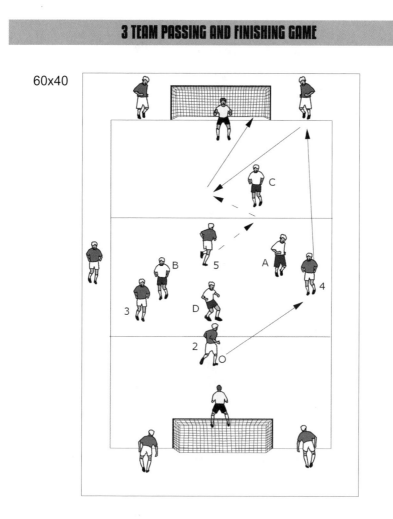

1. Three team game with fourteen players. When one team scores they stay on, the losing team goes off and the winning team plays the outside team.

2. The ideal setup is 2 keepers and 13 outfield players, but you can arrange it based on the number of players you have at the practice. There are many variations on this theme.

3. **Competitive:** Play the game over a certain time period and see which of the three teams scores the most goals in that time.

4. In this set up it is best if the outside support players have only one touch to pass the ball back in, which will usually set up a one touch finish to goal.

60x40

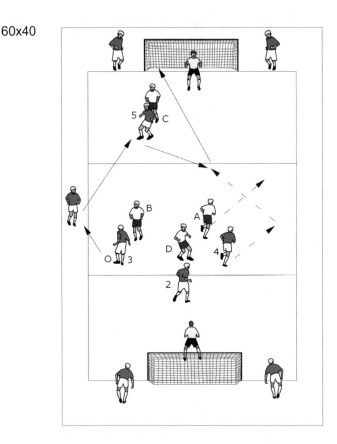

1. **4v4 with keepers**. In the example, we have fifteen players to work with, so five on the outside, one of which will be a keeper for the outside team when they get into the game.

2. Here (B) blocks a pass to striker (5) from (3) so the outside player is used in a support position to get the ball to (5). (4) loses the defender (A) and gets a ayoff pass from (5) to score. This is just one example of many situations that can be created by this game plan.

3. **Coaching Points:**
   a) Quality of Passing
   b) Quality of Support and movement off the ball
   c) Quality and Speed of Finishing
   d) Effective Team Play

50x18

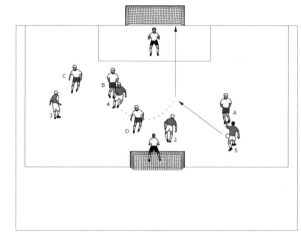

GAME OBJECTIVE: QUICK ONE AND TWO TOUCH FINISHING IN THE BOX

1. **Coaching Points:**

   a) **Quality of Passing** - Concentrate on the weight, timing and angle of the pass. Under-hit the pass to draw the receiver to the ball and into a position to shoot and get free of the defender. This technique is used to allow the receiver to hit a one touch shot at goal. Weight of the pass must be light to allow this. This is the opposite to what coaches normally tell a player (don't pass the ball short or under- paced because it can be intercepted). Above: a short under-hit pass draws the player towards the ball to get free from the defender and, half turned with a side on stance, hit a one touch shot.

   b) **Positioning and Crossing Technique** - (creating width to cross).

   c) **Balance in Attack** - (near post / far post / middle of goal). Positioning from crosses, timing of runs (late and fast), changing of positions to move defenders, angles of runs, contact on the ball.

   d) **Finishing Technique** – One touch finishing if possible as a lack of time on the ball in the box usually requires this.

   e) **Anticipation of Rebounds** - off the goal, off the keeper or off defenders.

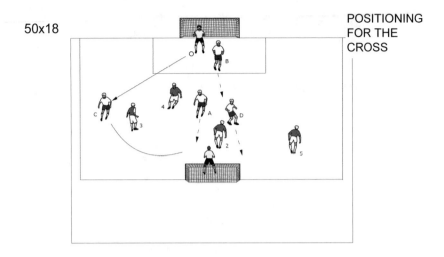

50x18

1. The keeper plays the ball wide and the attackers get in position to meet the cross near post, far post and centrally behind them for the pull back.

2. Try to finish one touch.

3. The game is constant attacking play both ways.To make it competitive, count the number of goals scored. Encourage the players to shoot on sight.

4. With constant quick transitions from defending to attacking, and attacking to defending, this exercise improves the concentration of the players in these key situations.

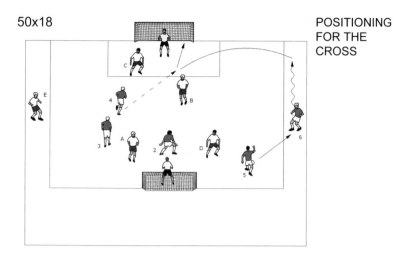

1. **Progression:** Introduce 2 players on the outside who stay outside the playing area. No one can tackle them so they are guaranteed to get a cross in.

2. This could be a quick play session focusing on crossing and one touch finishing, the emphasis being on a two touch maximum in wide areas to ensure a quick cross into the scoring area.

3. Players know they only have 2 touches when it goes wide so they work quickly to get into position, expecting the early cross.

4. This should improve quick decision making as everything is done at pace.

30x30

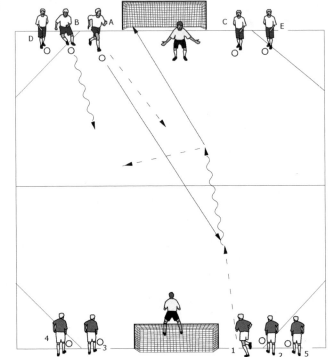

GAME OBJECTIVE: QUICK FINISHING THEN
ATTITUDE TO DEFEND

1. (A) passes to (1) and (1) has to score as quickly as possible.

2. (1) then becomes the defender for the next attack from another lettered player. (B) now attacks (1) and tries to score.

3. Players will forget to defend. "Punishment" is 5 push ups when they forget.

4. Keep the score of the game to keep it competitive.

5. **Coaching Points:**
    a) Quick attack
    b) Quality finishing
    c) Instant Mental Transition from attacking to defending

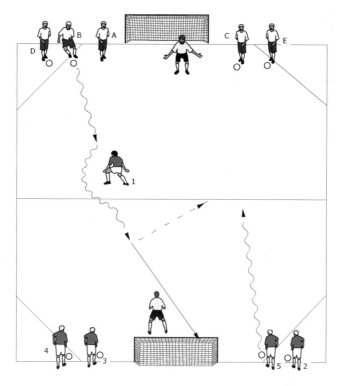

30x30

1. (B) has the choice of shooting early from distance before being challenged or dribbling around (1) and shooting at goal as above.

2. As soon as the 1 v 1 is over, (5) makes a run to attack and try to score quickly. (B) must recover back quickly to try to stop him.

3. Keep the tempo up and encourage the players to attack with pace.

Working with fourteen players (or less), we build the session up from no opposition to 1 v 1's up to 6 v 6's with various practices developed within the session. Work on attacking or defending play. Iif attacking, encourage lots of shots on goal. If defending, work to prevent shots and regain possession. Over the course of the session you may count the goals each team scores so they have an overall competitive challenge.

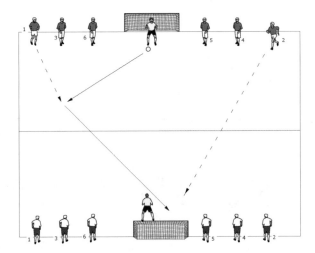

GAME OBJECTIVE: QUICK FINISHING INTRODUCING SMALL SIDED GAME TEAM PLAY

1. A teammate, or the keeper in this case, passes to (1) who shoots at goal following any rebounds in. Only one player going from each side to start. The other group do the same practice at the same time. Make it continuous.

2. **Progression:** In Two's same delivery from the keeper (as above). Variations can be:
   a) Keeper to (1) who shoots or lays off to (2) who shoots, (1) follows in for rebounds.
   b) Crossover run between (1) and (2), one player shoots, the other one follows in.
   c) (1) on the ball makes a diagonal run across, stops the ball for (2) to strike at goal. Timing of the runs is important.
   d) (1) and (2) make crossover diagonal runs, keeper throws to (1) who crosses for (2) for a header or shot.

30x20

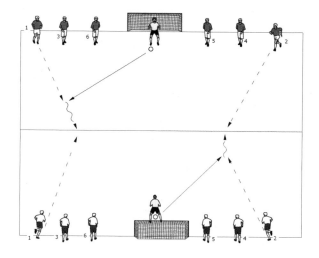

1. Going both ways at the same time. Start with one player from each side.

2. **Progression:** In Two's the other pair are effectively passive defenders in the spaces. Each pair must work out movement and shooting around and through the other pair.

3. Players need to be more inventive in thought and movement. Try things; overlap, pass and shot, give and go, pass and shot, take over, pass and shot and so on.

4. The coach can call out different numbers so the matchups are different.

5. **Coaching Points:**
   a) Alertness to receive
   b) Working combinations
   c) Early shot
   d) Accuracy before power in shooting, but trying to achieve both
   e) Follow in for rebounds

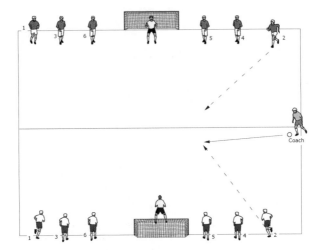

Competitive: Introduce defenders and go back to working in ones from both sides, one being a defender and one being an attacker. The first part of the session was designed to get players comfortable on the ball and gain success from their endeavors by shooting and scoring goals.

1. You can work on attacking or defending in a 1 v 1 situation.

2. Have both teams practice both attacking and defending in a 1 v 1 situation against different opponents on each team.

3. If the defender wins the ball he can attack and score a goal.

4. Players can work with their keeper (this can help the keeper's ball skills).

5. Intensive work when you are in play but rest periods for a good recovery.

30x20

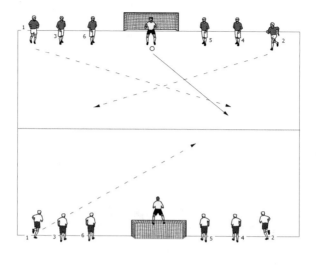

<u>2 v 1's</u>

1. Spread out to make it difficult for the lone defender. Players can begin with diagonal runs.

2. Working crossovers, overlap runs, 1 – 2's, decoy runs, diagonal runs etc.

3. You can coach attacking or defending.

4. Have both teams practicing both attacking and defending in a 2 v 1 situation.

5. **Progression: 2 v 2's**, play to a finish. Both teams can score. The coach can serve the ball in for a 50 / 50 challenge to gain possession or rotate who gets the ball first.

6. Encourage players to try to score quickly, otherwise they need to work combination plays between them.

30x30

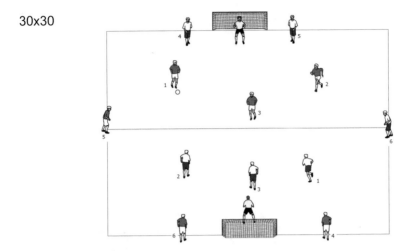

Develop the session by introducing a 3 v 2 situation. If the two defenders win the ball they can try to score on goal. Develop into 3 v 3's as above.

3 v 3's using Support Players

1. Support players have one or two touches, which creates quick layoffs for shots from the end players and quick passes from the side players. Support players can move to help the angle of support.

2. You can time each game or rotate the teams after each goal. If it's by a goal scored the scoring team can stay on for an extra game as a reward and only the opponents change. Vary the touches on the ball as the games progress. Two touch means players need to make quicker decisions in limited space.

3. **Progression 1:** Move to a 4 v 4 Have support players rotating with the inside players as they receive a pass. Outside in, inside out.

4. **Progression 2:** Finish with a game of 6 v 6 plus keepers. Work a 3-1-2 or 3-2-1 system of play. The area is very tight for 6 v 6 but it is good for the players and emphasizes the need for a good first touch. The session is particularly good for goalkeepers, who get lots of work and are involved the whole time.

25x20

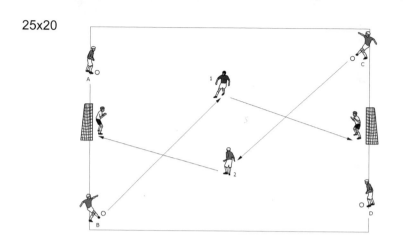

GAME OBJECTIVE: RECEIVING, TURNING AND FINISHING AT PACE

1. Players are side on to receive. (B) serves to (1) who receives, turns and shoots. Simultaneously, (C) serves to (2) who performs the same movement.Turn both ways. (1) then receives from (D) to attack the other goal, and (2) receives from (A). Work the shooters hard for a few minutes then rotate the players. Both players work both ways alternately. Try to make it two touch, one to control and turn and one to shoot.

2. Introduce another player who becomes the shooter and the other two players are the receivers. Shooter positions between the receivers and works a position to receive one touch from them to shoot at goal. For example: (B) serves to (2) who lays the ball off one touch for the shooter to shoot. Then (C) passes to (1) who does the same going the other way.

3. **Coaching Points:**
    a) Server must serve with precision and pace.
    b) Receivers need a tight first touch to turn and shoot or lay off for teammate to shoot if going in two's.
    c) Quick feet to get into position to receive and shoot or lay off to teammate.
    d) Hit the target (accuracy before power).
    e) One touch quick finishing where possible.

25x20

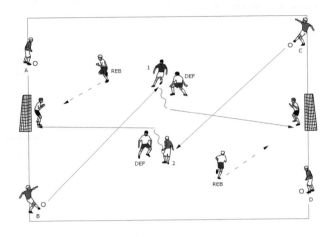

1. **Progression 1:**
   a) Have rebound players positioned near each goal to keep the keepers on their toes.
   b) Introduce passive defenders.
   c) Fully competitive 1 v 1's. If defenders win it they can try to score.

2. Here we have introduced passive defenders (D) and also rebound players (R) to put the keeper under more pressure

3. Rebound players can link up with strikers. For example, striker receives and turns, plays a one touch give and go with the rebound player and shoots at goal, with the rebound player following in.

4. Now take out the rebound players and have 1 v 1's so if defenders win the ball they can score. Players go out in pairs and one has to receive and try to turn and score while the other has to defend and try to win the ball and score in the other goal.

5. 1 v 1's going both ways at the same time.

6. **Progression 2:** 2 v 2 's receiving and turning and trying to score, but only going from one side at a time due to limited space.

25x20

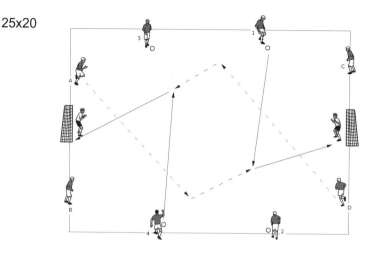

GAME OBJECTIVE: ONE TOUCH FINISHING
UNDER PRESSURE

1. The field dimensions are two 18 yard boxes (36 x 44). One striker attacks from each end simultaneously, Server 1 to striker A and server 4 to striker D. Each striker then joins the diagonally opposite line. Once they have finished, B and C attack and 2 and 3 serve.

2. **Coaching Points:**
    a) Timing of the runs off the pace and the type of pass.
    b) Quality of the one touch finish.
    c) Hit the target (accuracy before power).
    d) Follow up for rebounds.

3. **Progression:** Attack in pairs with players working as a unit, playing 1 – 2's, one touch shooting with rebound positioning.
    Variations on service: a) driven low, b) chipped for header, c) delivered at different angles. Keep the practice short and sharp as it would be in the box in an actual game. Strikers' runs should be as late and as fast as possible.

25x20

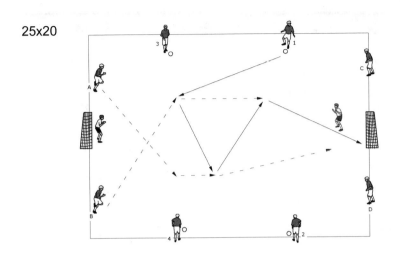

1. Attacking in two's from one side at a time. (A) and (B) perform crossover runs then (1) passes to (B). (B) plays a 1 -2 or give and go with (A) and shoots at goal. (A) follows the shot in for any rebounds.

2. The players then go to the other side to attack the opposite way. (C) and (D) work the same move going the other way with a pass from (4).

50x40

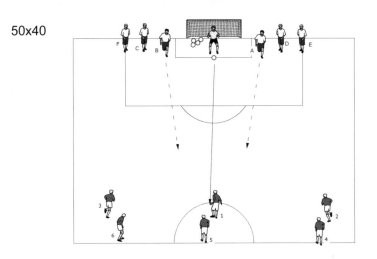

GAME OBJECTIVE: DEVELOPING COMBINATION PLAYS AND FINISHING

1. The keeper starts the exercise by throwing the ball out to an attacking player.The first thought of the attacker is "can I shoot?" If not, the three attackers should try to create a position between them to score a goal. As soon as the keeper has thrown the ball, two defenders close down the space quickly.

2. Try to isolate one defender and create a 2 v 1 situation. (1) passes to (2) and makes an overlap to create a 2 v 1 against (A).(2) moves inside with the ball and either passes to (1) to cross or uses the run as a decoy to come inside to shoot or pass to (3) and create a 2 v 1 there against (B). (3) takes up position accordingly.

3. Don't run in straight lines. Make diagonal runs to move the defenders around.For example, (3) may make a diagonal run across (2) and take defender (B) out of position, thus creating space for (1) to shoot or run with the ball. If (B) doesn't track (3), he may be free to receive a pass and shoot.

50x40

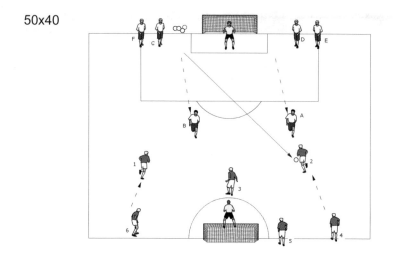

DEVELOPMENT

1. **Progression:** Introduce TWO keepers and TWO goals to make the set-up more realistic.

2. With larger numbers, have the players rotate on and off in 3 v 2 situations. You may need to make a 4 v 2 situation depending on the ability of the players. You can show them tried and tested ways to create overload situations to begin, then let it go free and see them use their own imagination. Rotate players so defenders get the chance to be attackers and attackers to be defenders.Rotate keepers.

3. **Competetive:** Each team has 10 chances to attack and score. Which team can score the most goals?

4. **Coaching Points:**
    a) Quick Attack
    b) Quick decisions
    c) Working Combinations (overlap, give and go, take-overs, decoys etc)
    d) Quality Finishing (accuracy and power)
    e) Rebounds

50x40

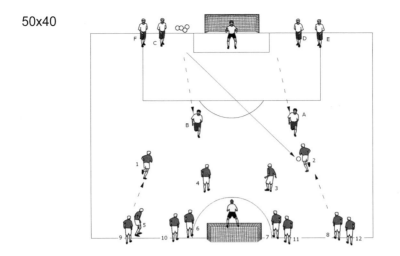

1. Introduce keepers and increase the size of the goals to make the set-up more realistic. You can have keepers in from the beginning also if you wish.

2. With larger numbers, have the players rotate on and off in 4 v 2 situations.

3. You can show them tried and tested ways to create overload situations (as previously shown) to begin, then let it go free and see them use their own imagination.

4. Rotate players so defenders get the chance to be attackers and attackers to be defenders. Rotate keepers.

TRANSITION TARGET GAMES

40x40

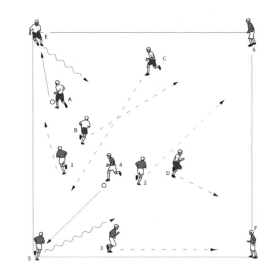

GAME OBJECTIVE: SWITCHING PLAY AND
QUICK TRANSITION

1. Two teams with a ball each playing to targets. Once they get to one target they must work to get the ball to the other target. As a player passes to a target he must change over with the target player who comes into play. As (4) passes to (5) and switches position, already the other players have spread out to attack the other target.

2. Teams play through each other and must have awareness of where their own players are and where the other team is as they pass through them. Emphasize a good first touch out of their feet to set up the next pass or passing first time to a teammate.Always stress to the players that they must look before they receive the ball. Ensure as the ball is transferred from one end to the other that all players get a touch on the ball before it gets to the next target.

3. As the ball is passed to the target and the target player brings the ball out with a good first touch, the other players must already be positioning themselves to be in support to transfer the ball to the other target, this means spreading out width wise and length wise to make themselves hard to mark.

4. Make sure they don't turn their backs and run away but keep looking at the ball and open their stance up to receive a pass or at least offer an option. Show movement across the field as they break out, diagonal runs for example (C & B), no breaking in straight lines (easy to mark). Introduce opposition so the two teams play against each other and make it competitive by keeping score.

40x40

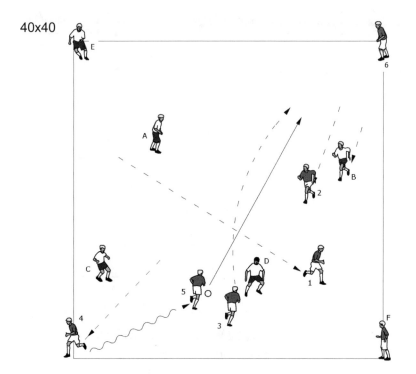

1. (4) becomes the new target player with a pass to (5).

2. (5) runs the ball out and (1) and (3) make diagonal runs in front to lose their markers and get free to offer passing options to (5).

3. (2) runs away from in front of the target to get free to receive a pass, or take defender (B) away from the space (5) is running into.

4. In this situation the best action for (5) is a pass to (3) who can easily score by a pass to target player (6).

5. **Coaching Points:**
   a) Quick Transition from inside to outside player
   b) Immediate Support positions of team mates (movement off the ball)
   c) Decision making by the player on the ball (pass, run, dribble)
   d) Score a goal by passing to the other target player

40x40

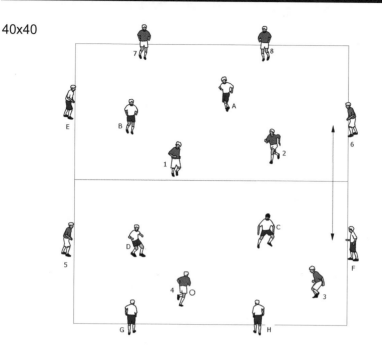

GAME OBJECTIVE: IMPROVING MOVEMENT OFF THE BALL

1. **Rules:**
   a) Players must pass the ball to their target players to score. To score again they must work the ball back into their own half of the field to be able to return.
   b) Target players have two touches, as do side players.

2. **Coaching Points:**
   a) Creating Space by running off the ball to receive or to help a teammate receive.
   b) Quality of Passing; long and short to targets and to teammates.
   c) Support play: working angles and distances, switching play using the side players.
   d) Receiving and Turning in tight situations and dribbling in 1 v 1 situations.
   e) Quick decision making is required in this session because the numbers are small, the area tight and the transitions rapid.

3. **Progressions:**
   a) No restriction on touches then 3, 2 or 1 touch, but only if it is on.
   b) All outside and target players one touch only where possible.
   c) Switch with target players as they receive the ball.
   d) Switch with outside players
   e) Use the opponent's target players as support players.

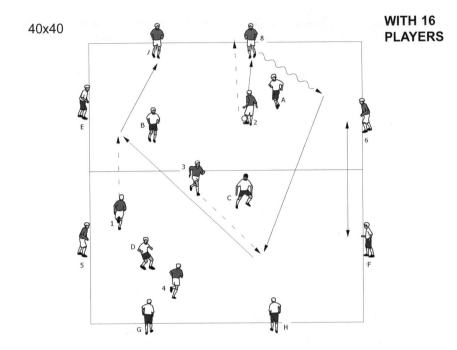

1. Here is an example of the transition and movement off the ball to make it happen. I have left the defensive players static in this situation to highlight the movement of the attacking players.

2. (2) passes to target player (8) who brings the ball back into the playing area.

3. (3) makes a run into the other half of the field on the blind side of (C) to receive the next pass. They need to get the ball into that half to be able to score.

4. (1) makes a forward run into space to receive the next pass off (3) and passes to target player (7) who can start the play again.

5. (1) switches with (7) and becomes a target player for the next phase of play.

6. You can play the same game with 12 players. To get the inside players more involved as individuals reduce the size of the game from 4 v 4 to 3 v 3 so the responsibility of each player then becomes greater to have an influence on the game, as there are fewer players.

1. **Observe the Attacking Team:** Recognize their movement off the ball for example to work the ball into their own half see if the players make runs early in there as soon as the ball is at a target, some should support short and some long so the target has choices.

2. **Observe the Defending Team:** see if they are sucked to the ball or they recognize runs off the ball and track players making runs away from the ball into the other half.

3. To lessen the workload and keep everyone involved have players switch with targets and outside side players when they pass to them.

4. **Elements of play the target game teaches:**
    A) *Attacking as a Team and as Individuals*
        a) Creating Space by running off the ball to receive or to help a team-mate receive.
        b) Developing quick support play working angles and distances incorporating switching play using the side players.
        c) Passing long and short to targets and to teammates.
        d) Receiving and turning in tight situations and dribbling in 1 v 1 situations.
        e) Lots of touches on the ball for the players in this practice.
        f) Quick decision making is required in this session because the numbers are small, the area tight and the transitions rapid.
    B) *Defending as a Team and as Individuals*
        a) Pressurizing players on the ball to regain possession.
        b) Supporting pressuring players and tracking runners off the ball.
        c) High pressure to regain possession in the attacking half to be able to go straight to the target to score.
    C) *Transitions from defense to attack and attack to defense*, quick decision making and improved concentration as the switch occurs. Interchanges of positions between inside players, targets and side support players.
    D) As a coach you can work in this session how to defend properly as individuals and a team or how to attack properly as individuals and a team.

CONDITIONS TO CHANGE THE FOCUS OF THE GAME

1. No restriction on touches then three, two or one touch but only if it is on to do so.
2. Introduce neutral player so 5 v 4 overload in the middle if possession isn't kept easily.
3. Interchanges of players outside to in, inside to out as they pass the ball observing the quality of the pass and the first touch of the receiver or performing a crossover.
4. Have one teammate at each end so you are attacking both ends but once you have passed to one target you keep possession and must try to get to the other target. You can't go back unless the opposition win the ball then you get it back, only then can you go back to the same target.
5. To lessen the workload and keep everyone involved have players switch with targets and outside players when they pass to them. This causes a constant transition of players and focuses the players concentration.
6. The team can only score if they get an overlap, crossover or 1 – 2 in during the build up.
7. No talking so players have to rely on their own vision to play.
8. Players move into the target zone to receive (timing of run and pass) so we don't play with actual targets, different players can then become the target player.
9. Man – Marking – Have the players man mark so they must track a player when they haven't the ball and they must lose their marker when they have the ball. This is a good test to see who is working hard and who isn't as they have a designated job to do. You as a coach can see who works to get free of their marker and who works hard to prevent the the player they are marking get the ball.
10. To improve the speed of thought reward a successful one touch pass with a goal. To score a goal by passing to the target player now reward this with three goals or 3 points.
11. This session is particularly good as a midfield play practice session as you can liken the start when the ball is at a target as it being a target defender passing it in and to get to the other side through midfield to the other target who is now a striker. Then this target player maintains possession and the team can go the other way, the target striker then becomes a defender for the attacking team starting the move and the other target becomes the striker to pass the ball to. So it is consistent movement end to end with the attacking team from a defender into midfield to a striker.
12. The team in possession can pass back to the opponents target players to help keep possession of the ball. Liken this to passing back to the keeper in a game situation.

With 15 Players

1. Make it a 3 team game for 15 players (for example). Each game lasts 10 minutes, the winning team stay on the field as a reward. You can vary the positions of the outside players, 2 target players at each end and one support player on one side or one support player on each side, one target player at one and end and two at the other and so on.

2. To make it technically a 10 v 5 game have the team in possession able to play with the outside team. They are trying to score at one end, so these players are on their side but they are also able to work with the side player and the two target players of the other team, using them as support players also.

3. This encourages them to pass back and open the play up and not be focused on just playing forward all the time.

40x40

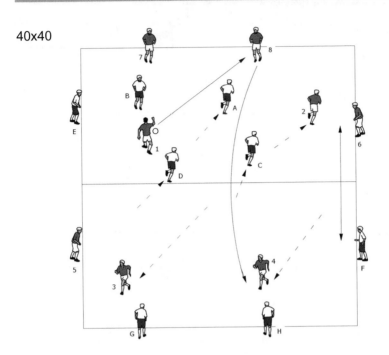

1. This is an example of what to look for on the defending side of things.

2. Here the ball has been passed to the target (8) and a goal scored. The defenders are ball watching and not seeing the runs "off the ball" of their opponents.

3. The idea of getting the ball back into the other half before they can score again when in possession highlights these kinds of moments you need to identify in a game situation.

4. (1) plays the ball to target (8) to score. (2) supports the next pass short and at a wide angle, and (3) and (4) make runs into the other side of the field and off the ball to get free and receive a pass. Defenders are all ball watching and not looking at these runs and so (3) and (4) get free. At the same time you can say it is getting it right offensively.

5. The coach has to identify these situations and stop the game and show the set up and ask the defending players what they need to do.

40x40

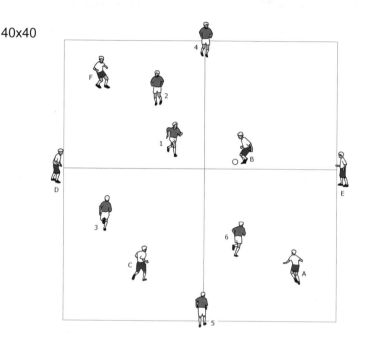

GAME OBJECTIVE: IMPROVING TURNING AND CHANGING DIRECTION

1. **Rules:**
    a) Attacking different ends of the zone. Helps transition and dribbling and turning on the ball (a goal is scored by passing the ball to a target and keeping possession).
    b) Outside players change with inside players who pass to them.
    c) Once a goal has been scored at one end, the team has to score at the opposite end. They can go back to the player who scored the goal and use this player as a support player only. If possession changes and then the team wins it back they have the choice of going to either goal until they score one goal, then they attack the opposite goal again.

2. **Observations:** Players get a rest by passing into the target and transitioning positions. This maintains quick quality play because players don't get too tired (quality drops because of fatigue).

Coaching Points:
    a) Quality of pass by inside player
    b) Quality of first touch by outside player to move into space quickly and set
       up a new attack.
    c) Players must change direction as they gain possession of the ball
       because they are defending one end then suddenly attacking at right
       angles to where they were defending. Aids quick decision making.
    d) Attitude to attack quickly is important so players must be positive in mind
       and action.
    e) Individual 1 v 1's
    f) Team passing and support play.
) Everything done at pace.

40x40

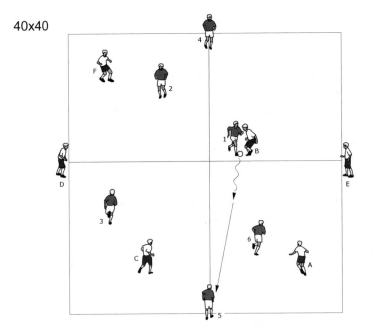

1. (1) wins the ball off (B) and immediately must change direction to score a
     goal.

2. Two directions to go; to target player (4), or target player (5); here the
     choice is a pass to target player (5).

3. Defensively the letters team now needs to focus on defending in a different
     direction to which they were attacking, and thus defending two sides.

80

40x40

1. (1) passes to (5) to score a goal and takes (5)'s place as a target. (5) brings the ball out and attacks the opposite goal.

2. If the pass to the outside target player is a long one and the run is very long for the passer then the closest teammate to the target players can change places with them for efficiency and quickness.

3. Here (3) and (6) move off the ball to support (5). (2) is already in a good position to receive a pass.

4. Once a team gains possession they can score in either end.

5. If (B) wins possession, then (5) wins it back, (5) can pass to either of the outside target players to score a goal.

6. Players should try hard to keep possession and work the ball from one end to the other, scoring goals at both ends.

40x40

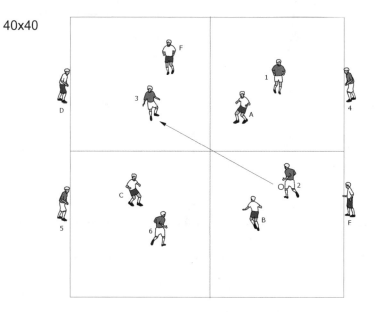

GAME OBJECTIVE: QUICK PLAY, PASSING AND SUPPORT

1. Quick continuous attacking play which is good for anaerobic fitness. Breaking one way, passing to an outside player and switching positions, inside player out, outside player in, then attack the other side of the zone.

2. **Coaching Points:**
   a) Technical ability on the ball in 1 v 1 situations.
   b) Quick Transition in attack - As the transition between players happens (for example (3) changes with (5)), the numbers team must get the ball to (4) as quickly as possible.
   c) Observe the movement of (1), (2) and (6) in terms of their support positions as the directional change takes place. They must move in anticipation to find space to help the player on the ball as the switch occurs.
   d) Observe also, as the change occurs, the positions of the defending team. Has the decision been made quickly enough who presses the ball? Are the other defensive players supporting and covering and tracking runners off the ball?
   e) Improvement of quick decision making, tight control because the spaces are small to play in, and thinking in advance due to the switch in direction of the play.You can also work on the defending players.
   f) The coach must learn to look away from the ball and observe what may happen next before it happens.

40x40

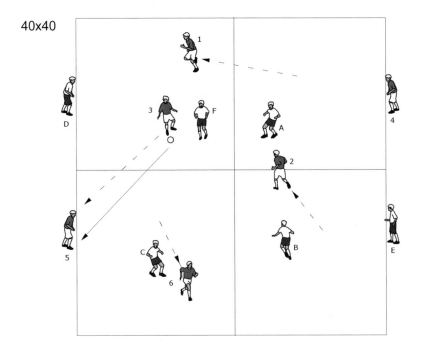

1. Here (3) passes to (5) and (3) leaves the area. As the ball is traveling to (5), (1), (2) and (6) must get into a position to help (5) as early as possible so, (5) can make a one touch pass to any or all of them. Thus (5) already has three pass options.

2. Their movement is OFF THE BALL and away from their markers.

3. Of course the defenders will move to compensate but for the sake of what I am trying to show it is easier to get the point across by showing the movements of the attacking team only.

4. The attacking players in the actual practice may get free like this anyway if they time it correctly.

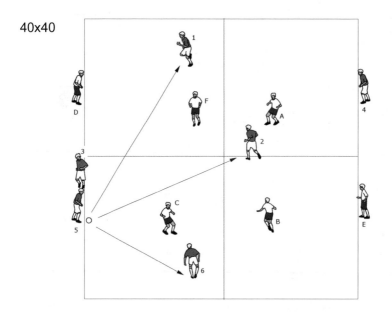

40x40

1. Here we have the resulting situation where we show the positioning of the attacking players each being free to help (5) by getting open for a pass.

2. (5) may elect to run with the ball but there are at least three options available for a pass if needed.

3. (5) may even elect to play a long pass straight to (4) on the other side of the field if the pressure from (C) is not fast enough. You may then ask the closest player (in this case player 2), to be the switching player instead if (5) passes directly to (4).

4. You could then work on defending in this game. However, you should focus on defending or attacking, not both, as it can be confusing for the players..

40x40

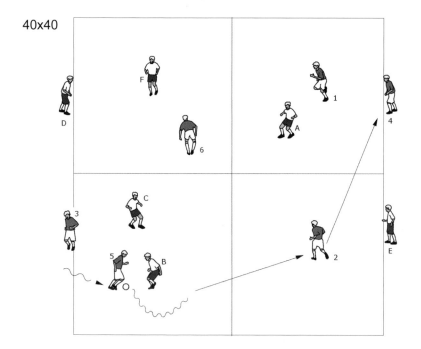

1. Here (3) passes to (5) and they switch positions, (5) dribbles past (B) and scores a point in a 1 v 1 and plays a quick pass to (2) who passes to target player (4) who scores another point and this player (4) has to quickly attack the other way again.

2. You could argue that the best place to dribble is in the opponent's half, but in this small area you can encourage players to do it all over the field.

TRANSITION GAMES
WITH GOALS

60x40

COMFORT
ZONES
5 yds wide

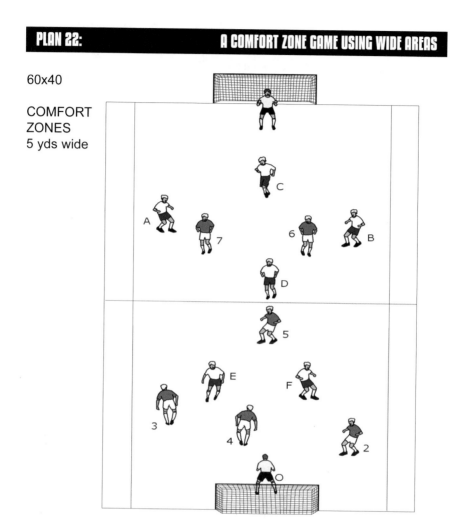

GAME OBJECTIVE: TO ENCOURAGE PLAYERS TO USE WIDTH AND OFFER AN AREA TO PLAY WITHOUT PRESSURE

1. If a player breaks wide into the outside channel on either side of the field and is in possession of the ball this player cannot be tackled. Defenders are not allowed into the channel.

2. The players on the team in possession of the ball can run the ball into the channel or have it passed to them into the channel.

3. This condition plants the seed in the mind of the players to immediately play with width when in possession. Numbers for this game can be 3 v 3 and upwards.

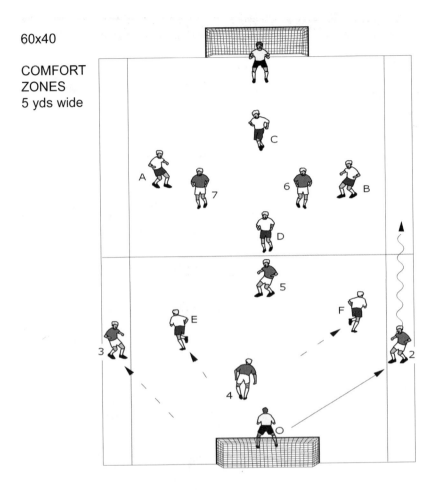

60x40

COMFORT
ZONES
5 yds wide

1. (E) and (F) can "shadow" the outside players.

2. Only one player allowed in the channel on one side at any one time when the team is in possession of the ball.

3. Players can only stay outside in the channel with the ball for a few seconds then must make their move inside either passing it in or dribbling it in or it becomes too false a set up.

4. **Coaching Points:**
   a) Create space wide when in possession of the ball
   b) Building play from the back
   c) Using width to attack

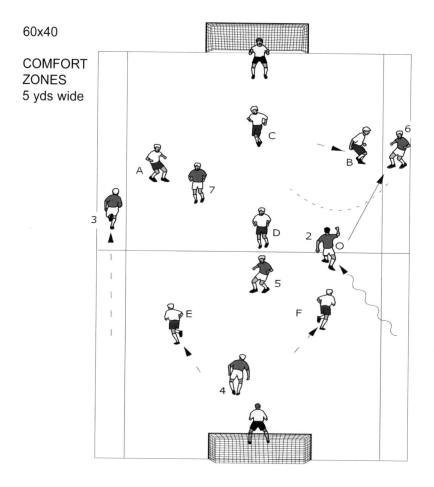

60x40

COMFORT
ZONES
5 yds wide

1. Striker (6) makes a run outside into the channel to offer an option of a pass for (2). Defender (B) can only "shadow" this run. By allowing the striker (6) to receive wide in the channel and have no pressure it again encourages the team to use width in attack but this time in the attacking half.

2. (3) is already in the channel on the other side and continues the forward run and is another option for a pass, as are the players inside the actual field of play.

3. Who (2) passes to can depend on the reaction of the opponents and who is left free to receive a pass or (2) may just attack with the ball with a forward run or dribble. (2) decides to pass the ball wide into the path of the run of (6).

60x40

COMFORT
ZONES
5 yds wide

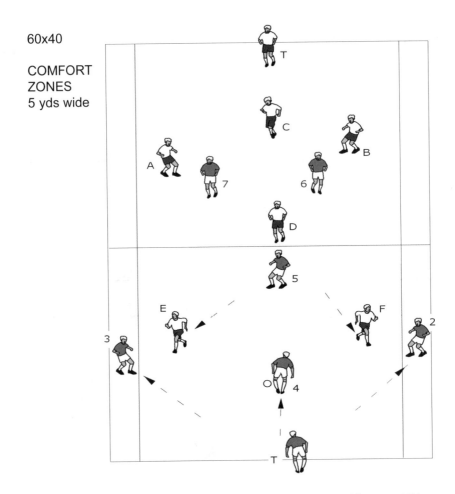

1. The letters team work the ball to their target. When a goal is scored this way, the ball possession is transferred to the other team and they must immediately break wide to offer options.

2. Here the two defending strikers (E) AND (F) have broken wide also so there is space for (4) to receive in the middle. Encourage the play to be wide or through the middle depending on the positioning of the opponents.

3. **Develop:** The wide areas can be used to practice certain moves the players have been taught, especially at the younger ages where they need to be able to practice them without pressure. This allows for them playing in a game but also doing the move without pressure. For example a certain dribble can be practiced then the ball dribbled in or passed into play.

60x40

GAME OBJECTIVE: SWITCHING PLAY AND
USING WIDTH IN ATTACK

1. Using three goals as reference points award one point / goal for scoring in the central goal and two points / goals when scoring in the wide goals to encourage the players to spread the play using width in attack. If it is tight down one side, encourage them to switch the play and go down the other side.

2. Using the goals on the field, award a point / goal if they play through the goal, again encouraging the use of width in attack. Players can dribble or pass through these goals. If it is tight down one side and they can't score because the other team is defending well, players must spread out on the other side to receive the ball with the idea that the team can score a point / goal by passing or dribbling through the other goal on the far side of the field (thus switching the play).

60x40

1. **Coaching Points:**
   a) Creating Space by movement off the ball
   b) Open body stance to receive and change the play
   c) Quality Passing to maintain possession
   d) Using Width in Attack to score through the outside goals
   e) When, why and where to Switch the Point of attack
   f) Scoring goals, especially in wide areas

2. **Progression:**
   a) Reduce the number of touches on the ball to speed up decision making
   b) Introduce keepers to guard all three goals (as above).

60x40

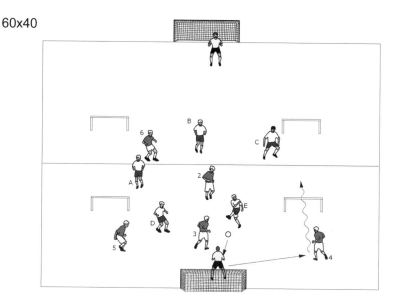

OBJECTIVE: CHANGING PLAYER MENTALITY FROM DEFENDING TO ATTACKING

1. Likewise this can be a transition from an immediate defensive mentality to an offensive mentality. (E) shoots at goal and the keeper gets possession and immediately (4) breaks wide to receive and try to score in the small goals.

2. **Coaching Points for Attacking:**
   a) Create Space to receive or to help others receive
   b) Immediate mental shift from defending to attacking
   c) Maintain possession
   d) Score quick goals

3. The opposite happens where (E) must immediately try to stop (4) from scoring. In this case (E) has not changed from an attacking to defending mentality and allows (4) to score and maintain possession.

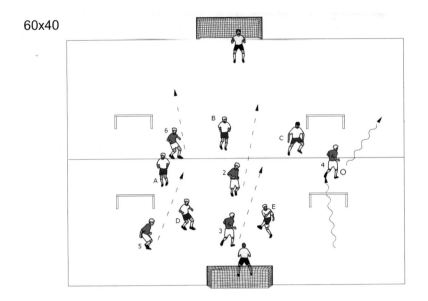

1. The numbered team attacking have scored in the small goal and are now looking to score in the big goal.

2. The whole team pushes up quickly from the back, leaving opponents offside.

3. Defending team needs to recover back and try to win back possession.

40x40

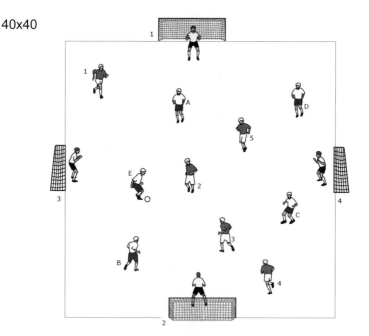

GAME OBJECTIVE: CHANGING THE POINT OF ATTACK AND QUICK SHOOTING

1. Numbers team attacks goals 1 and 2. Letters team attacks goals 3 and 4.

2. **Coaching Points for the game:**
    a) Creating Space with movement off the ball
    b) Quality Passing to maintain possession
    c) Awareness of when, why and where to Switch Play
    d) Transition between attacking and defending as an individual and as a team
    e) Changing the direction of attack on winning the ball
    f) Scoring goals

3. **Progression:** Introducing keepers to put greater emphasis on the act of scoring and finishing.

4. **Coaching Points for Attackers:**
    a) Quick Play
    b) Positive Attitude to shoot
    c) One and two touch finishing

40x40

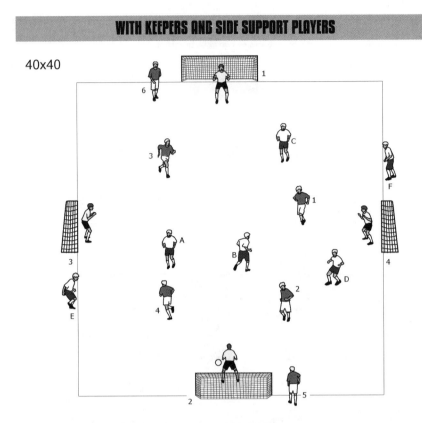

1. 4 v 4 game, numbered team attacks goals 3 and 4, lettered team attacks goals 1 and 2. If you score a goal you retain possession as a reward , the team's own keeper serves the next ball in. This session can be done with small goals and no keepers.

2. a) **Attacking Play** – Get quick strikes in on goal, quick movement and support play with the means to switch play if necessary.
   b) **Defending Play** – Quick pressing to regain the ball, support play working as a unit to regain possession.
   c) **Transition** – Concentration from attack to defense if your team wins or loses the ball. It's a small area so wherever the ball is lost the other team has a quick chance to shoot.

3. Defenders have to work quickly to stop them. Attacking and defending differ- ent areas means concentration must be good when the ball changes hands. Players rotate in when they are ready.

40x40

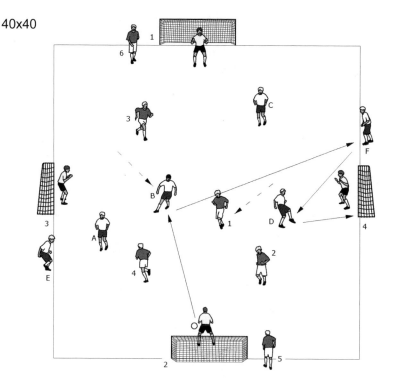

Coaching Points:
    a) Quick accurate passing
    b) Quick support play by teammates
    c) Positioning to get off a quick shot
    d) Positive attitude to score
    e) Preparation for one or two touch finishing (feet and body in position to receive the pass to shoot quickly due to little time and space)
    f) Follow in for rebounds

40x40

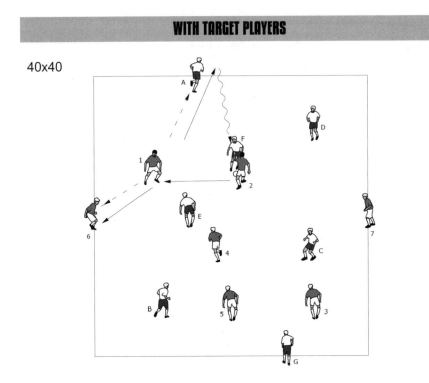

1. We now have target players to pass to, so the game is continuous and more of a possession game. Targets have one or two touches to keep the game moving quickly. Vary the number of touches depending on the level of play.

2. **Progression:** Have the player who passes to the target player switch positions with him so there is constant rotation of players to keep everyone involved.

3. An example of a play above: (A) passes to the target player (F) and runs outside to be the next target, (F) brings the ball inside to try to score at target (G) but loses possession to player (2), who immediately passes to (1) who scores with a pass to target player (6) and then switches with that player.

4. Once they score by passing to a target player they have to try to get the ball to the other target player opposite to score again. They can use the same target player as a support player. If possession changes hands and then the team wins it back, they can then go to either target player to score.

Time the break to get a shot in. Ten seconds max.

Working both ways alternately. Good conditioning session also.

GAME OBJECTIVE: COUNTER ATTACKING
AND QUICK FINISHING

1. **16 players**. Players make two passes amongst themselves in midfield then pass it into the striker and three players support quickly. Recovery runs from defenders cannot begin until the ball has been passed into the striker.

2. **A 1 v 1 situation**. Pass to space for (1) to come off the defender and turn. Three players break quickly to support, two central and one wide. One defender makes a recovery run to help (4 v 2). It is a 4 v 2 situation and the striker has to get free of the defender and create space for the attacking support players. Working both ways for both teams alternately to have the opportunity to have successful attacking situations for both teams. Once one attack is over the next begins in the other half of the field to keep the game dynamic.

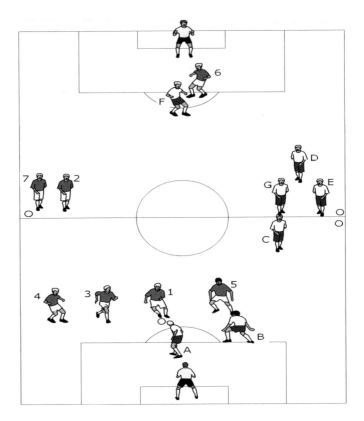

1. Here we have the positions of the players after the recovery runs of defenders and also the attacking support runs of the attacking midfielders, a 4 v 2 advantage. Change the setup to 2 v 1, 2 v 2, or 1 v 2 up front to offer new challenges to the players.

2. Working both ways alternately. This game teaches the players to be quick and decisive in their decision making when they have the chance to break in an overload counter attack.

3. **Progression:** Have defenders recovering from both sides of the field for a more balanced defensive set up. Also have attacking players breaking forward from both sides of the field.

4. **Coaching Points:**
   a) Quick interplay and fast service to strikers
   b) Quick break and movement of support players
   c) Attitude to score
   d) One and two touch play where possible to get in a quick finish.

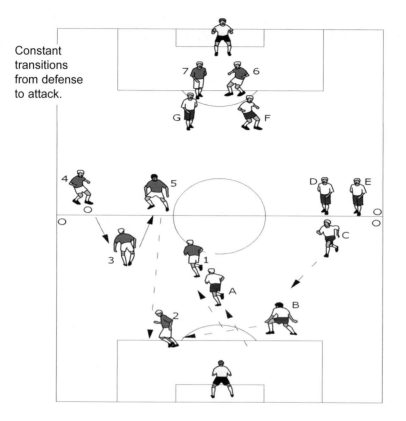

Constant transitions from defense to attack.

1. **Example of a play:** Movement of the strikers; here (1) goes short to receive to feet and takes (A) with him, creating space behind for the diagonal run of (2) who goes late and fast to get away from marker (B) and try to get a shot at goal or link up with another attacking midfield player. Timing of the run and the pass is important.

2. Late and fast can mean (2) receives it in front to go on to shoot at goal having escaped (B) marking. In too early and (2) may receive the ball with his back to goal and (B) behind. In this case, it is more likely that (2) will have to link up and work with a midfielder and will not get the immediate shot off.

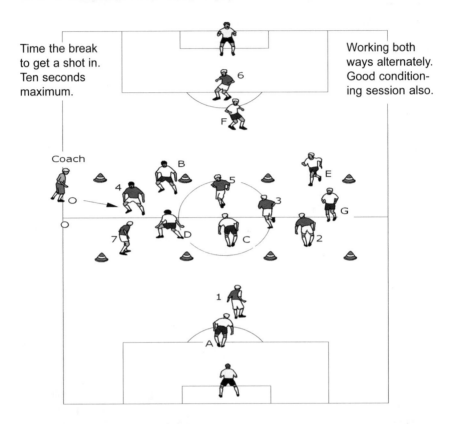

Time the break
to get a shot in.
Ten seconds
maximum.

Working both
ways alternately.
Good condition-
ing session also.

GAME OBJECTIVE: QUICK BREAK AND TRANSITION FROM ATTACKING TO DEFENDING

A Directional Game: Creating overload situations for quick break play.

1. The team in possession makes three passes in the marked midfield area then passes into the striker. Two midfield players break quickly to support (making a 3 v 1 overload in favor of the attacking team) and / or one defensive midfielder can recover (3 v 2).

2. This leaves a 5 v 3 situation in the middle zone in favor of the other team who are currently defending (if no recovering midfielder is used to begin).

3. If the defenders win the ball or the keeper receives it, the ball is played quickly into the middle zone (to a 5 v 3 overload) where they make three passes then get the ball into the striker to attack quickly in the other direction.

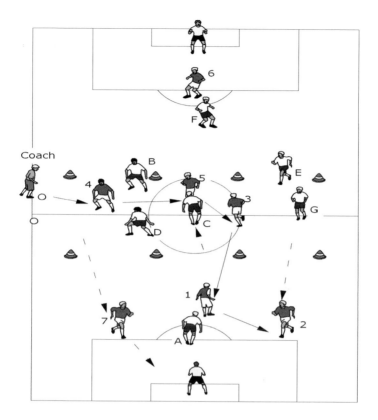

1. **3 v 1 attack**. Vary attacking and defending numbers to present new challenges to the players.

2. **Progression:**
   a) Players can run the ball in as well as pass it in
   b) Introduce a recovering defender from the middle zone who can then act as a link player attacking the other way if possession is regained.

3. **Coaching Points:**
   a) Quick Breaks in attack.
   b) Rapid Passing and Support play.
   c) Early and quick shots on goal.
   d) Quick counter attacks going the other way.
   e) Quick recovery runs of previous attacking midfielders (now defenders) as possession changes.

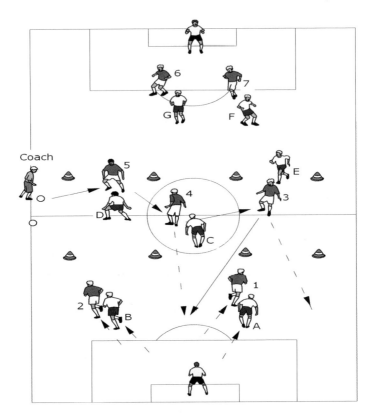

1. **Now 2 v 2**, strikers can move defenders around, and work split runs to get a midfielder in. (2) takes (A) away, (1) takes (B) away from the space and here midfielder (3) plays the ball into the path of midfielder (4). If (B) stays in the space then (1) is free to receive.

2. The midfield can just pass the ball in when it's on, it could take three passes or maybe only one.

3. While a team is attacking one way the strikers and midfielders of the defending team must move players around and make themselves available and free from marking, in anticipation of a change of possession so they are ready to break quickly the opposite way.

4. The previous attacking midfielders are now defenders and have to recover back quickly into the middle zone. If a striker is closer to the middle zone, he can recover back for an advanced midfield player.

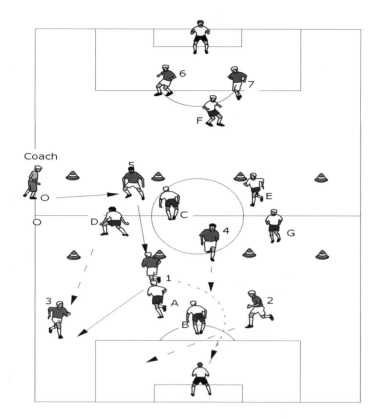

1. **Still 2 v 2**. The often used method of attack here is for the striker to go short to receive to feet, half turn and play the ball wide for an attacking midfielder who breaks forward and gets a cross into the box. Now it is the secondary movement of the strikers to get into the box once the first link up has been made that we need to focus on. Players should attack all the important areas in and around the box: near post, middle of the goal and far post, all done as quickly as possible, emphasizing speed in attack.

2. (2) near post, (1) far post and midfielder (4) in the middle around the edge of the box.

PLANNING

ATTACKING TEAM

1. Midfielders must get the passes in and then break quickly and support the strikers as the ball is played into them. Midfielders can run the ball in or pass it in for another player to run onto. Vary the support players from here based on where the immediate space is.

2. Strikers must get free from their markers to receive the ball and link up with the attacking quick break midfielders or turn and attack depending on the positions of the defenders.

3. They need to score in a certain time. Decrease the time allowed as they improve.

4. Vary the number of players in striking positions as you develop the session. Start with one, then two, and have these two linking up together to develop. Movement off the ball to create space for themselves and for each other.

5. As soon as the move breaks down, the attacking midfield players who joined in with the strikers need to get back to the midfield area they vacated. You can also coach them to recognize it may be a striker who is closer who makes a recovery run back to fill in for the midfielder who may have ended up deep in the attacking third of the field. Nearest player= shortest recovery route back.

6. The idea is to overload the attack so we gain success from the session in an attacking sense.

DEFENDING TEAM

1. Recovering players get back quickly to counter the quick attack.

2. Vary the number of defenders already in position and those recovering as you build up the session to change the challenges for the teams.

3. Midfielders and strikers of the team without the ball are ready to break quickly should they win it back in the defending third. They need to be constantly on the move, getting free from opponents to receive the ball once the keeper or a defender gains possession of it.

4. When the defending team wins the ball and it is played into midfield it may be a defender who joins in and goes all the way into the attacking third. Players can pass it in or run it in. Make sure a midfielder drops back into a defensive position in the defensive third to cover for this. This encourages the players to rotate positions and develop more freedom in their positioning on the field.

GENERAL OBSERVATIONS

1. Maintain the overload situations in midfield as the transitions take place from defense to attack to ensure you get the session working effectively so there is constant transition from attack to defense and defense to attack, both happening at pace.

2. Eventually open the game up into an actual scrimmage and see if both teams have adopted the quick break mentality you have been trying to teach.

3. Now it is equal numbers in all areas so it will be a good test for the players to see if they can make it work.

Developments for the transition game
1. 1 v 1 in each attacking and defending zone and 4 v 4 in the middle zone (numbers can vary here).

2. Big overload to gain success in the attacking play, three attacking midfielders and one recovering defender making a 4 v 2 overload.

3. 1 v 2 or 2 v 2 in the attacking and defending zones with fewer players in the middle zone but still equal numbers there. Midfield can run it in now. Work on the movement of the two strikers to create space and move the defenders around.

4. Allow a midfield player from the middle zone to drop back into the defending zone where his team has regained possession to provide help in the link up play (distances may prevent a good long pass from the back directly to midfield, depending on the age group being coached). Defenders can't follow them in so this gives a better chance for the attack to build quickly.

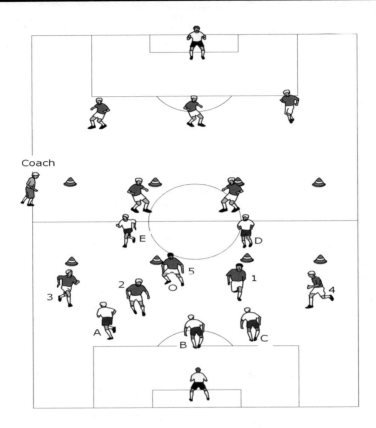

GAME OBJECTIVE: TEAM TRANSITION FROM DEFENSE TO ATTACK

Three teams of five players so you always have a 5 v 3 overload. Here the numbered team attacks. The defending team leaves two players in the middle zone. If the defenders win it or the keeper gets the ball it is immediately transferred to the middle players (D) and (E) and they attack the third team with the help of (A), (B) and (C). You can work how to attack in a 5 v 3 and / or how to defend in a 3 v 5 situation.

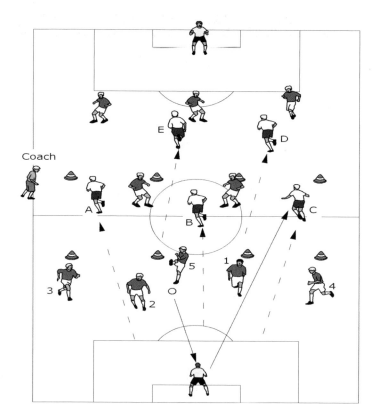

1. **Coaching Points:**
   a) transition from defending to attacking
   b) Quick break attack
   c) Finishing with a shot at goal
   d) Transition again

2. The numbers team have attacked. (5) shoots and the attack is over. (1) and (5), the closest players, drop back into midfield. The letters team now becomes the attacking team going the other way.

3. Encourage the teams when they win possession to break quickly and attack with pace. Always a 5 v 3 offensive situation to help the attacking teams.

75x50

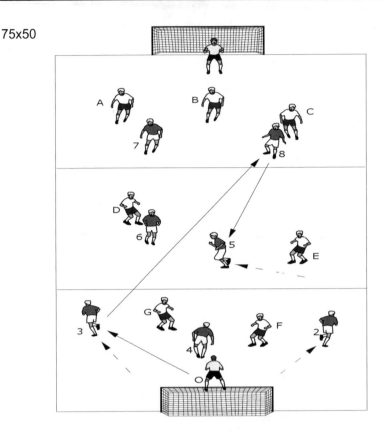

GAME OBJECTIVE: DEVELOPING TEAM PLAY THROUGH THE THIRDS OF THE FIELD

1. Start with a 7 v 7 and a 3 v 1 overload in each end third. Go to a 3 v 2 when they are comfortable (8 v 8), with the players developing play but staying in their own third to emphasize team shape through the units.

2. **Coaching Points:**
    a) Creating Space as an individual and as a team
    b) Quality Passing
    c) Playing and transitioning through the thirds from the back
    d) Support Positions of teammates, movements off the ball and exchanging positions on the field through the thirds
    e) Positive attacking play as a team
    f) Scoring Goals

75x50

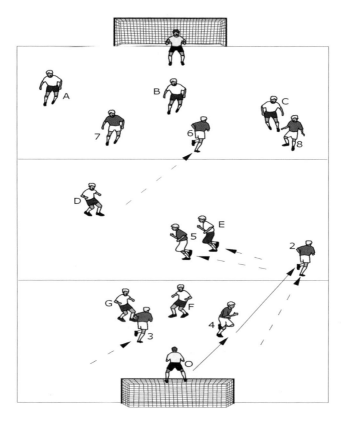

1. Now we are transitioning between thirds and as a defender changes the balance in midfield from a 2 v 2 into a 3 v 2, a midfielder then moves into the attacking third to change the balance from a 2 v 3 into a 3 v 3.

2. (5) clears the space for (2) to bring the ball forward. (4) and (3) cover across behind the field to support and be in a good position to cover should the move break down. This is clearing the space in front of the ball and filling in behind the ball.

3. (6) makes a run into the attacking third to become another target for (2) to pass to.

4. If the player can't go forward and has to play it back, make sure the players behind the ball get in positions where they are free to receive it and able to support the player on the ball.

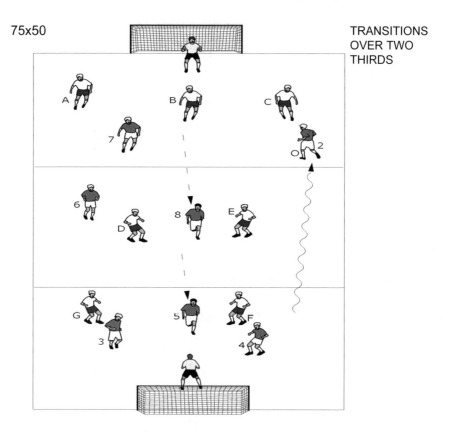

1. (2) on the ball may run over three zones with the ball. If and / or when the move breaks down and the opposition wins the ball, (5) can replace (2) and (8) can replace (5) so each player gets back the team shape by the shortest route. This encourages particularly the fullbacks to attack down the flanks as they know they don't face a 50 yard run back in a game situation because a teammate will cover for them. It may result in only a 10 or 15 yard run initially, saving energy and time.

2. This method of playing gives **FREEDOM** to the players. You can encourage the players to communicate with each other as this is happening, for example (2) runs forward with the ball and instructs (5) to be prepared to cover.

3. Players change back to their positions as soon as they can within the game. They can run the ball in, pass it in, or pass it in to a runner from their own zone.

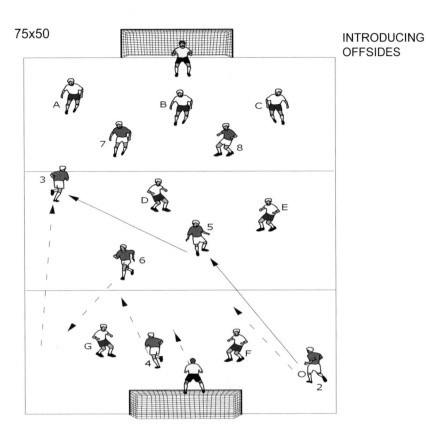

75x50

1. Player (2) passes the ball into the middle zone to (5), (3) moves up from the defensive zone to the middle zone to support. This type of transition movement is important because it allows players to move freely between the zones knowing they will have a teammate covering for them.

2. **Progression 1:** Have offside from the defensive third of the field. (2) passes the ball forward and both (2), (4) and the keeper push up. In terms of the opposition this rapid movement and transition makes it difficult for them to pick players up, to read what your team is doing.Usually (D) would be marking (6) (who can cover) but now has to think about marking (3). This means defenders aren't just defenders, midfielders aren't just midfielders and attackers aren't just attackers.

3. They work to help each other through the three units of the team and are free to mix the game up.This is total soccer, played to encourage the free movement of players.

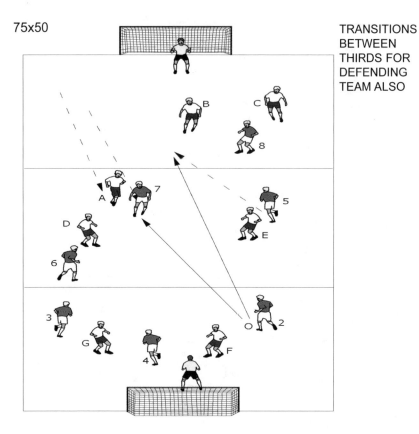

TRANSITIONS
BETWEEN
THIRDS FOR
DEFENDING
TEAM ALSO

1. **Progression 2:** Players can transition back into zones from the attacking third to the midfield third, the midfield third to the defensive third. Defenders still cannot move between zones. Example: striker moves back into the midfield third (to receive to feet or free space for someone else to move into) and a midfielder moves forward into the attacking third.

2. **Progression 3:** Allow defending players to track attacking players into the other zones. When this happens the defender follows the striker going short, creating space behind for another striker to move into or a midfielder to break forward into. Ultimately open the game up so the players have no boundaries to use for focus and see if they can work out how to keep that balance and shape on an open field of play.

75x50

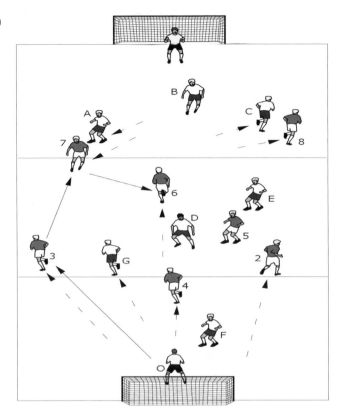

1. **Progression 4:** Introduce a three, two then one touch restriction to see if the players can work more quickly and still gain success. This speeds up their decision making in the game.

2. When playing one touch, be realistic. Sometimes a pass may be so heavy the player needs two touches. Use one touch only if it is on to do so.

3. We have introduced many progressions to work up to letting the game go free and observing if the players can incorporate into the free game situation all they have learned.

4. Here quick play by the numbers team puts the letters team at a disadvantage using one and two touch passing, not allowing the defending team to get close to intercept by moving the ball quickly. (6) has a shot at goal having lost marker (D).

117

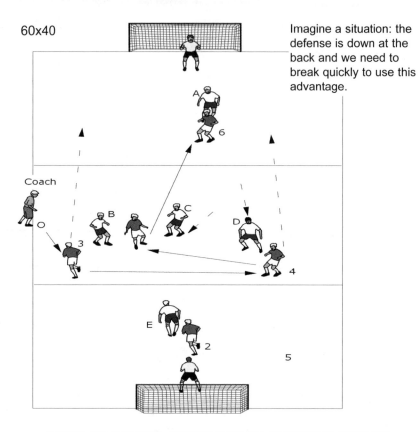

60x40

Imagine a situation: the defense is down at the back and we need to break quickly to use this advantage.

Coach

GAME OBJECTIVE: QUICK BREAK, COUNTER ATTACK AND FAST FINISHING

1. This is a condensed version of the full field game.

2. This is for a team playing 8 v 8 with 12 players in the squad. 3 v 3 in the middle, 1 v 1 at either end. Coach passes the ball in, team in possession plays 2 or 3 passes then must get it to the striker. 2 midfield players support to make a 3 v 1 in the attacking third. Focus is on the quick break from mid-field. They must score quickly. This leaves a 3 v 1 going the other way in the middle third as we transition the play.

60x40

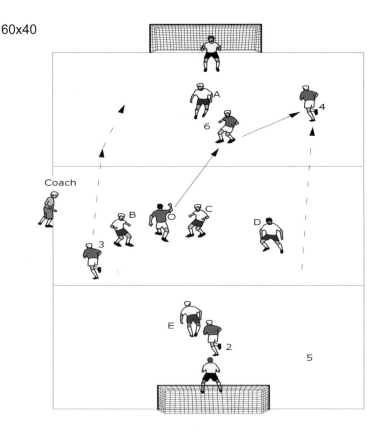

3. A 3 v 1 in the attacking third now should ensure a quick attack and shot at goal. They have to score in 5 seconds (smaller field). Three lettered players are ready to go the other way in the transition with the 3 v 1 advantage. Defending letters team in midfield cannot recover back and track so there is always an overload. Players beak into spaces where they can support both sides of striker (6).

4. **Coaching Points:**
   a) Quick Breaks in Attack.
   b) Rapid Passing and Support play
   c) Early and quick shots on goal.
   d) Regains of the ball and quick counter attacks going the other way.
   e) Quick recovery runs of previous attacking midfielders (now defenders) as possession changes.

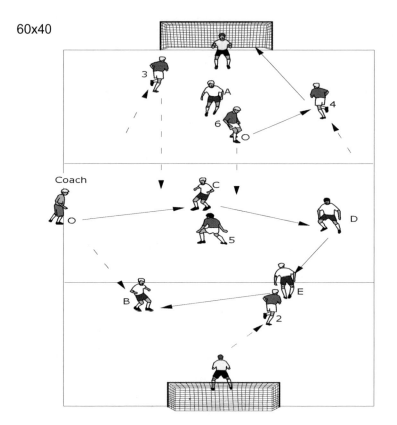

60x40

Coach

1. Striker (6) plays the ball to support midfielder (4) who shoots and scores. Support midfielder (3) follows in for any rebounds.

2. At this stage if the play is finished, the coach can pass another ball into the middle for the lettered team to use their overload situation to attack the numbered team quickly and before the numbered midfielders (3 and 6) recover back to challenge them. Here (B) is set up for a shot.

30x30

COMPOSURE
ZONES
5 yds wide

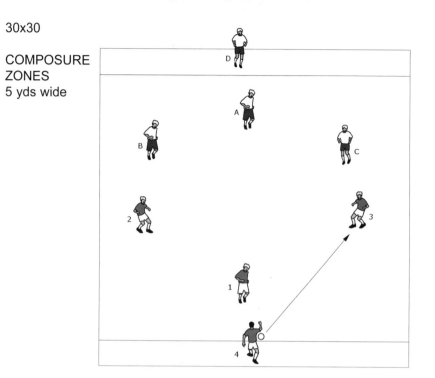

GAME OBJECTIVE: TEACHING COMPOSURE ON THE BALL
WHEN BUILDING PLAY FROM THE BACK

1. This is a small sided game introduction to a bigger game.

2. Players can bring the ball back into the composure zone where opponents can't track them.

3. This gives the player in the composure zone time and space to relax and play and build play from the back.

85x50

COMPOSURE
ZONES
5 yds wide

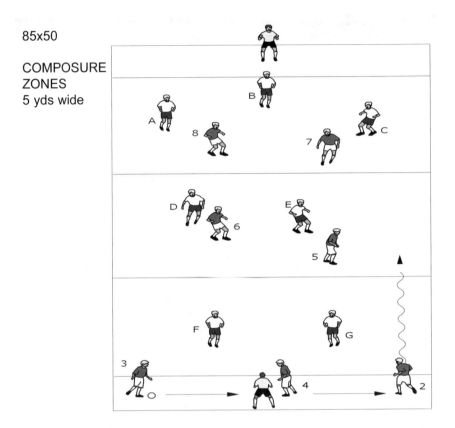

Coaching Points:
    a) Patience in possession and build up at the back.
    b) Recognizing the moment to play out of the back
    c) Run the ball out or pass it out
    d) Bring the ball back into the composure zone for safety, time and space.

1. Overload at the back.Two forwards can't encroach into the 5 yard compo-sure zone. Defenders pass ball across under no pressure until one is free to run it out. Attackers can then try to win it back.

2. Players stay in their own zone to keep their shape. Support in front and behind.

3. Open it up so players can move between zones.

4. Defenders can take the ball back into the composure zone for safety and this encourages spreading out and playing from the back.Be patient, keep possession; go forward at the correct moment.

5. Defenders – spreading out, running with the ball, passing the ball, support-ing the keeper, keep possession, decision making.
   Midfield – Receiving and turning, switching play, linking play, runs, keep possession, creating space, decision making.
   Forwards – As above, also supporting short and long, diagonal runs in front of the ball, holding the ball up, lay offs, dribbles \ shots, quick deci-sion making.

6. As ball advances, players at the back move up. Keep checking positions and shape of the team.

7. To get the full game started, have one team standing still and let other team play through them to get a feel for how to build up the play.

8. Develop this by having both teams with a ball each playing through each other where they are not under pressure of losing the ball.
   NB – If you have problems making this session work with equal numbers, build it up to the full team situation and organize 8 v 5 with only one forward, one midfielder, two defenders and a keeper in the other team.

PROGRESSION

1. Play offside from thirds.Players interchange between zones one at a time, always returning to the original set-up. Check the balance of the team with and without the ball. Create a 3 v 2 in midfield zone with player (2) moving up. Play the ball into attacking third and maybe player (6) joins in to make a 3 v 3.

2. Player (2) fills his place in midfield. On lose of possession, players either drop back in or you can develop the session to include pressing to regain the ball.e.g.If you are losing the game go full high pressure and leave three players in attacking third, two in midfield third and two in defensive third.

85x50

COMPOSURE
ZONES
5 yds wide

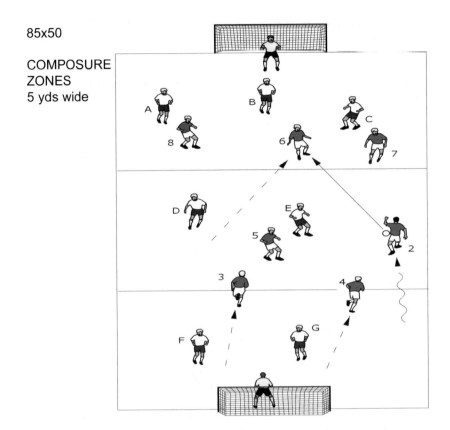

3. **Condition** – A goal can only be scored if all players are over the defensive third line. This reinforces keeping compact vertically.

4. Restrict the number of touches on the ball if players are able to do so to encourage quick passing and movement and to improve the speed of decision making.

5. Vary play by encouraging defenders to pass directly to the forwards. Midfield players can then support them facing the opponents goal (easier to support rather than receiving and having to turn with the ball).

6. If you have problems making the session work with equal numbers, reduce the game to an 8 v 5 situation using one forward, one midfielder, two defenders and a keeper on the opponent's team until the players are comfortable, then go into the full workout.

HEADING GAMES

30x15

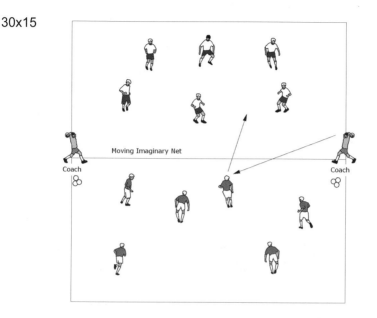

GAME OBJECTIVE: IMPROVING PLAYERS ATTITUDE AND ABILITY TO HEAD THE BALL

1. A coach feeds either team and players try to set up a header past the imaginary net (the line between the coaches) and make it hit the ground on the opponent's side.

2. The other team, if they keep the ball from hitting the ground, attempts to set up a header back over the imaginary net.

3. If the ball hits the ground past the line before the opponent player heads it back, the coaches move to this mark. Throw to each team in turn. If the ball is headed straight out at the side of the field the coaches go to where the ball was headed out and the opponents gain possession.

4. **Coaching Points:**
   a) Good service from the coach
   b) Heading the ball forward and down with pace to move forward (attacking headers) or over the top of players to score (defensive headers)
   c) Recovery (usually diving) headers by the defending team players before the ball hits the ground to regain possession.

30x15

GAME OBJECTIVE: IMPROVING HEADING AND DEVELOPING MOVEMENT OFF THE BALL

1. **Coaching Points of Heading:**
   a) Keep eyes open
   b) Move into the ball to head it with forward momentum where possible
   c) Head with the forehead, not the side of the head
   d) Get power from the hips and back, not the neck
   e) Arch the back and use the upper body for power
   f) Head high for defending headers, low for attacking headers

2. Players have to throw the ball and the next player must head it. The next player catches it.

3. Players cannot run with the ball but can run anywhere on the field without it.

4. Players must head the ball into the goal to score.

5. Coaching Points for the Game:
   a) Quality service
   b) Header with purpose and direction
   c) Support positions by teammates (for the pass to head or the header to catch)
   d) Attacking or defensive headers to suit where the ball is going (between opponents, over opponents)
   e) Attacking headers to finish and score on goal

30x15

GAME OBJECTIVE: IMPROVING ATTACKING AND DEFENSIVE HEADERS

1. Serve to a teammate who must head the ball into the other half. Three balls are used in the game so there are lots of headers. (4) throws for (2) who moves forward and onto the ball to help generate power.

2. Get height and distance and power on the ball (defensive headers). Count how many balls go in each half over a time period. The team with the most are the winners. Each player counts his own and adds them all up. You can have a team winner and an individual winner.

3. This is more a warm up game to get players into the action of heading the ball.

4. **Progression:** Try to head past the opponents and over the line to score. First team to ten goals is the winner.

5. Can head high and long over the opponents to score (defensive heading practice) and also head low with power between players (attacking heading practice) to try to head past the opposition. Opponents try to catch the balls and return the attack.

6. **Coaching Points:**
   a) Good service
   b) Aggressive headers in both attacking and defensive styles
   c) Scoring goals with headers

DEFENDING GAMES

70x50

GAME OBJECTIVE: TEACHING INDIVIDUAL AND TEAM PRESSURE

1. The game is designed to work on pressurizing the player on the ball, preventing a forward pass and ultimately winning the ball. The closest player has to pressure the ball. To score, a player has to make a pass from any where into the coach (or a keeper). The ball can be played in the air to the target's hands (to practice quality long distance lofted passes) or on the ground to feet (driven passes). All over the field, players must work hard to close people on the ball down quickly.

2. **Progression:**
   A) As a reward when a team scores a goal they keep possession so they play to the opposite goal to score. Previously they played to the same goal and the opposition got the ball when they scored.
   B) **Go to man** –marking so attacking players must get free and defenders must work hard to stop them from scoring. Applying high pressure as a team allows defenders to win the ball back early and close to the opponent's goal to score. Defenders must push up from the back.

70x50

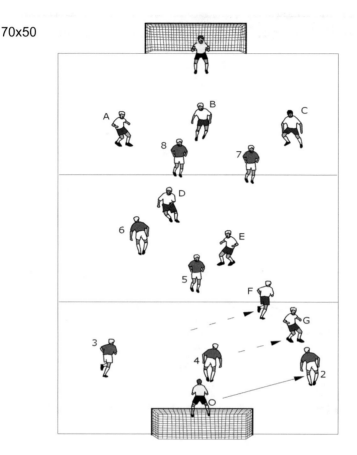

3. **Coaching Points:**
    a) Quick Pressure on the ball by the first defender
    b) Close Support for first defender from the second defender
    c) Deeper Cover from third defender
    d) Recovery runs from players in front of the ball
    e) Regaining possession

4. Here the job of player (G) is to pressure the ball as quickly as possible to win it back. (F) supports across, (G) shows the player on the ball inside towards (F) and between them they try to win the ball back quickly. (E) offers a balanced covering deeper position behind them.

70x50

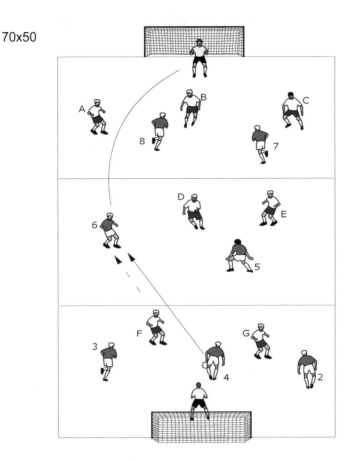

1. Players cannot go into the keeper's area.

2. Here (6) gets free of defender (D) and chips the ball into the keeper's hands to score a goal. Once this has happened a few times, players get the idea that they need to work hard to close opponents down quickly.

3. This game improves the urgency with which players close opponents down as they are so easily punished in this game if they don't.

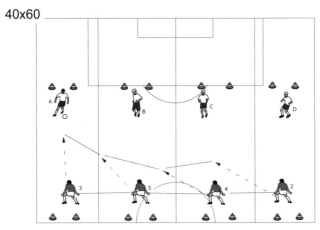

40x60

Players take their shape from four references: the rope, the zone the goal, the opposing players.

GAME OBJECTIVE: TEACHING ZONAL DEFENDING AS A UNIT

1. This begins as a 4 v 4 game working on zonal marking (marking space).Use a rope to tie the back four together so they must move as a unit and so they feel it. It can be a back four or a midfield four, the responsibilities are the same.There are four 5 yard wide goals on each team to defend.Teams can score in any goal at any time. Each team must work in a unit of four (or three with three goals to defend). Each goal is zoned off for a player to fill.

2. To keep a shape, players defend their own goals but must support their teammates to regain possession. Focusing on a goal of their own to defend helps them keep a sense of shape as a unit.They have to think about defending their goal, keeping their zone, supporting the pressing player and marking their own player who is in their zone. Players must try to maintain their shape and not be moved around by the opposition as they would if they were man marking.

40x60

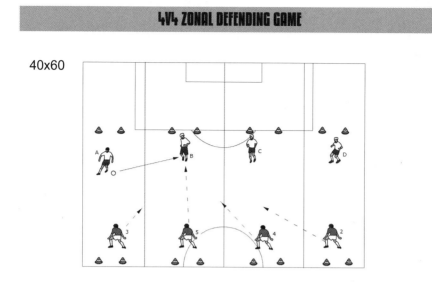

1. The ball is passed to (B) and the defenders adjust accordingly.They squeeze centrally behind the ball marker but stay close enough to close their immediate opponent down if necessary. For example (2) judges position by where the ball is and where the immediate opponent is so if the ball is passed to (D) there is time to close down and get there. Show the positions of the players in relation to their own goals. Can the opponent with the ball see the goal and score?

2. As the ball moves, each player adjusts to become the pressing player (if the ball goes to their immediate opponent) or a support player who judges position from how close they are to the ball.The closer to the ball, the more they mark the player. The further from the ball, the more they mark space. As above (5) is closest, (3) and (4) are next closest and (2) is the furthest away but still close enough to close down as the ball travels. Introduce offside to make it more realistic.

3. To establish where zones begin and end, place cones down to represent boundaries.

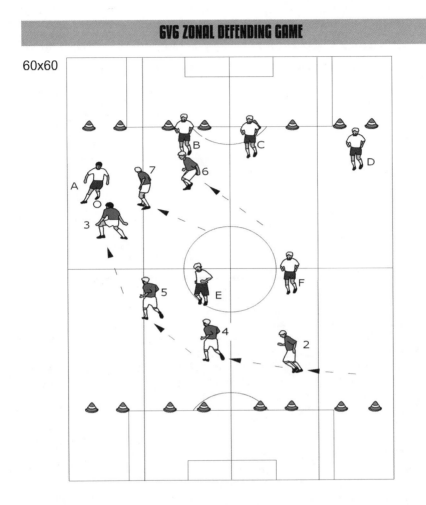

60x60

1. Introduce two more players per team. Each team can represent a back four plus two central strikers or a midfield four and two strikers. Again look to maintain a team zonal marking shape. (7) can double up. As (E) and (F) move across the back four they are passed on as they enter a new zone if there is someone to pass on to.

2. **Progression:** Introduce two wide players to each team to create a four and four. The attacking team tries to move players around, the defending team tries to hold their zonal shape but also win back the ball.

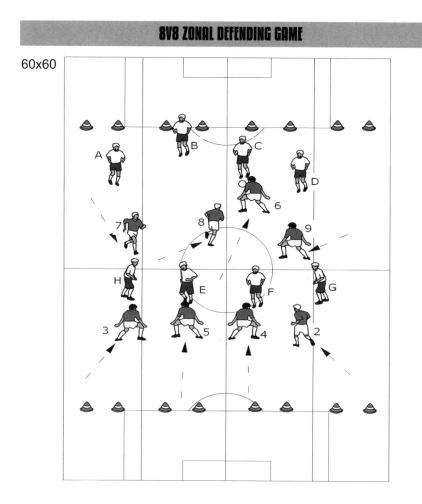

60x60

1. Now we have two 4 v 4 's with no free players. Players are still trying to maintain a shape while marking zones (spaces) but being aware of the immediate opponent's position.

2. (6) closes down the immediate opponent on the ball, (7), (8) and (9) close up around the ball but are still aware of their immediate opponents' positions.

3. **Coaching Points:**
   a) Quick individual pressure
   b) combination unit pressure condensing the space available around the ball
   c) regaining possession

60x60

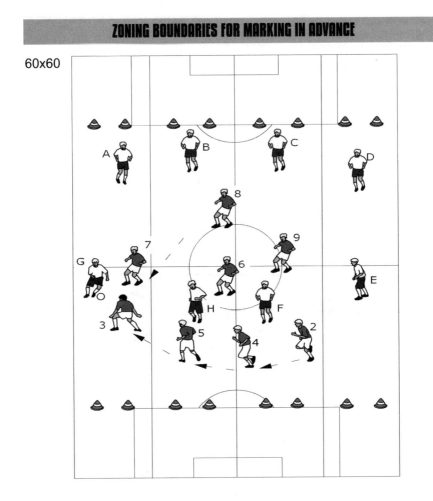

1. Each player knows where his responsibility lies in terms of zonal defending. Players mark players who enter their zone. Marking in advance of the ball means, for example, (2) is marking in advance of (E).

2. If the ball is passed to (G) from (E), (2) can try to intercept the pass or if he is not able to, at least stop (E) from advancing by closing down as the ball travels. (2) is still in a good position to defend, between the ball the opponent and the goal (inside the guiding triangle). Likewise (4) off (F) and (5) off (H). Eventually work a 4 v 8.

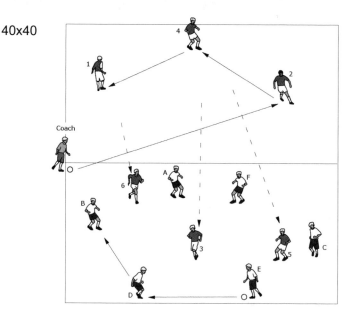

40x40

GAME OBJECTIVE: PRESSING AND TRANSITION

1. A **Transition game** creating 6 v 3 situations in both halves. The three defenders must win the ball back, then they can work it back to their own half of the field.They then move back into their own half and three defenders from the other team go in to try to win it back (another 6 v 3). While this is going on the three players left alone have a ball to pass to each other to keep them working, passing and moving until their teammates win the ball back. They then pass the ball to the coach who gives it to the remaining three players from the other team. Focus on what is happening on the ball, and what is happening away from the ball.

2. This prevents the three players left from standing still or just standing close to the half way line where, if they receive the ball, the other team doesn't have far to run to win it back. Even without the second ball these players should be spread out away from the action to give themselves time and space to receive the ball and keep it.

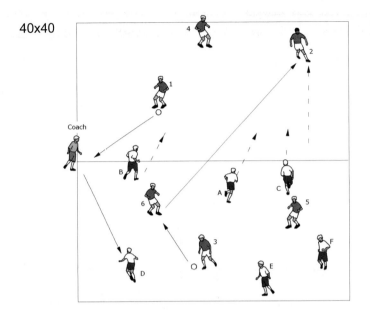

40x40

1. All players are working all the time. The three players must observe what is happening in the other half while passing their own ball around so that when their teammates win possession and bring it back into their own half they are ready to receive and also they recognize the time to play their own ball to the coach.

2. (3) wins the ball, passes to (6) who passes back into their own half to (2) who has dropped off to receive in more space. (3), (5) and (6) then recover back to their own half to try to keep possession.

3. (1) with the other ball passes to the coach who passes to (D). (A), (B) and (C) move into the other half to try to win it back.

4. **Coaching Points for Defending:**
   a) Quick individual player pressure
   b) Support pressure from the second defender
   c) Covering from the 3rd defender
   d) Regaining possession and quick transition

45x30

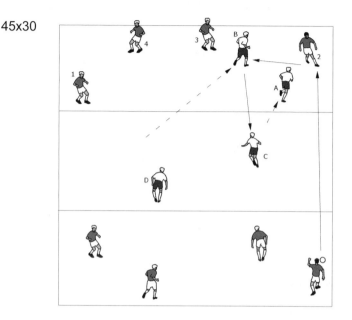

GAME OBJECTIVE: PRESSING AND WINNING POSSESSION

1. You can also work on the defending players and how best to win the ball back so the focus becomes a defending pressurizing game rather than a possession game. Here good pressure by (A) forces a bad pass from (2) and (B) regains possession.

2. **Coaching Points for Defending:**
   a) Quick Individual Pressure on the ball to force errors
   b) Close support (working as a pair)
   c) Regaining Possession

3. **Progression:** If the defenders win the ball they can take it back into the middle and the team who lost it sends two players in to win it back (becomes a 4 v 2 in the middle). (A) and (B) join (C) and (D) in the middle to try to keep the ball and the 2 closest players on the numbers team have to try to win it back. This keeps the game more continuous rather than having teams change zones when they lose the ball. Once they win it back and take it back into their own zone we go back to the 3 passes and change zones rule.

45x30

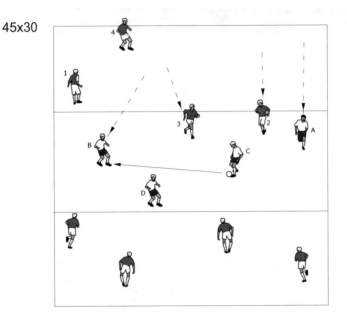

1. The numbers team has lost the ball and need to win it back. The letters team, on winning the ball, get it back to the middle and all 4 players try to keep possession.

2. Two numbers team players go into the middle to try to win the ball and get it back to their own area and create a 4 v 2 in their favor.

3. The middle team, when they win it, just have to try to keep it there until they lose it.

4. End line teams need to get at least 3 passes in then transfer it to the other end zone over the middle zone.

144

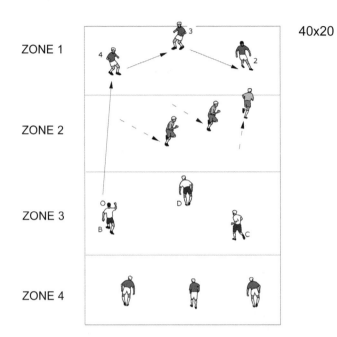

40x20

ZONE 1

ZONE 2

ZONE 3

ZONE 4

GAME OBJECTIVE: PRESSING AND DEFENDING AS A UNIT

1. Players must stay in their own zones.

2. Liken it to a midfield three unit in the middle of the field of play getting close together to stop a pass through them or forcing the player to make a pass over them. Making the attackers play the ball into the air means it at least is harder for the receiver to control than a ball on the ground.

3. As the ball travels from (4) to (3) to (2) the team in zone 2 travels across the field as a unit also. Here they get compact and close together, cutting down the space between them for player (2) to pass the ball through. The players in zone 3 need to move to open an angle up to receive but the defending players in zone 2 have made this difficult by their collective positioning.

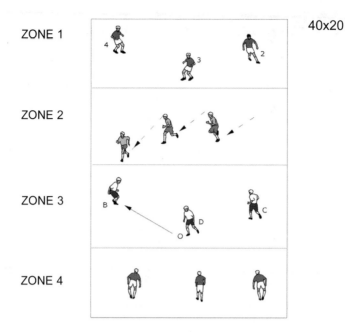

ZONE 1

ZONE 2

ZONE 3

ZONE 4

40x20

1. The ball is with (D) in zone 3 who has to work some passes with teammates to get the ball to the numbered team in zone 1.

2. The team in zone 2 has to try to stop them and win possession. They can shadow the passes but not encroach into the other team's zone. (D) passes to (B) and the three players in zone 3 close down the space in front of (B) to make it difficult to pass to the numbered team in zone 1.

3. The best option for (B) may be to pass to (C) who is free and in space. The three defending players in zone 2 must adjust across the field as a unit quickly to try to keep this player from passing into the numbered team in zone 1.

4. You can limit the number of passes a team has to make before they must try to pass it to another zone so the defending team have a chance to win possession. Otherwise, teams get bogged down just passing in the same zone many times. This forces the team in possession to move the ball quickly and take chances.

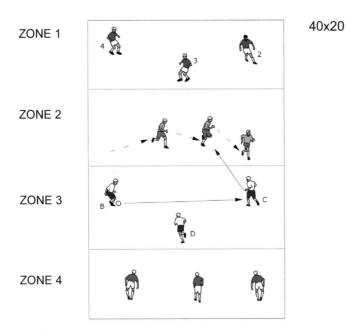

ZONE 1

ZONE 2

ZONE 3

ZONE 4

40x20

1. Here (C) tries to play the pass between the two defending players and the ball is intercepted. It may have been after a sequence of 4 passes and this was the last pass they were able to make and the ball had to be transferred to the other zone.

2. **Coaching Points for Defending:**
   a) Quick individual pressure: stepping into the passing channel or lane to intercept the pass.
   b) Group defensive pressure: 2 or all 3 players get compact as a group, closing down space as a unit.

3. **Progressions:**
   a) Restrict the number of touches on the ball of the attacking team, making it two touch play. This speeds up the play and speeds up decision making.
   b) Vary the number of passes required in each zone before the ball must be transferred to another team in another zone.
   c) Allow teams to make one pass before transferring the ball into the other zone if the best pass at that time is the long switching pass. This tests the defenders' speed of positioning.

60x40

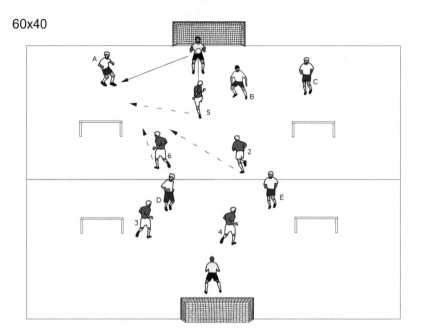

GAME OBJECTIVE: CHANGING PLAYER MENTALITY FROM ATTACKING TO DEFENDING

1. Each team can score in the two small goals in their own half and also score in the big goal in the opponent's half. Offer 2 points to score in the small goals and one in the big goals. Players can dribble through the small goals to score and then also keep possession.

2. The numbers team has attacked and scored in the big goal or the keeper has saved the shot and they immediately have to defend the small goals and their own big goal. This forces the numbers team to defend high up the field and in the attacking third of the field and forces them to change from a tactical attacking mentality into a tactical defensive mental attitude. Here (5) defends, trying to force (A) towards supporting defending players (6) and (2). If they win it here they have a great chance to score.

60x40

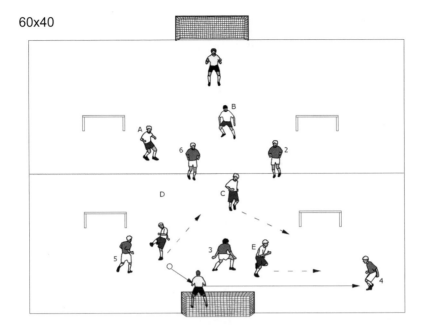

1. **Coaching Points for Defending:**
   a) Immediate Pressure: Individual defending close to the opponent's goal
   b) Team Defending in a high pressure way

2. Here (D) shoots and the keeper saves. (4) breaks free to receive and (E) who is now a defender protects the immediate small goal from (4), forcing (4) to come inside to the supporting defenders.

3. Likewise, if (5) broke wide to receive, (D) could close (5) down and protect the other goal on the other side of the field. In this case (D) supports (E) and (C).

4. This protecting of the immediate small goals sets in the players' minds the need to try to win possession early, DEFENDING FROM THE FRONT, and in the attacking third of the field, close to the opponent's goal. Hence strikers need to be taught how to defend correctly.

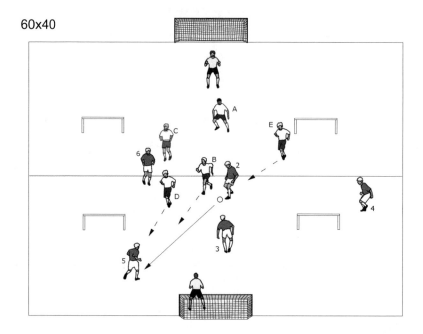

60x40

1. Even though the team in possession has gone past the two small goals they can still go back and score.

2. By allowing this development, this again forces / encourages the defending team to push out and press from the front.

3. Here (2) is well defended and can't pass forward so he looks for support behind. (5) drops off to receive and help. Dropping deep and behind a small goal can result in scoring a goal through the small goal.

4. Thus (D) must push on and offer immediate pressure on (5) to prevent this. The rest of the team pushes forward to support the pressing by (5) ensuring more defending from the front.

5. This also forces strikers, who are usually the closest to the ball in these situations, to defend quickly, often not a job they are good at or enjoy.

150

60x40

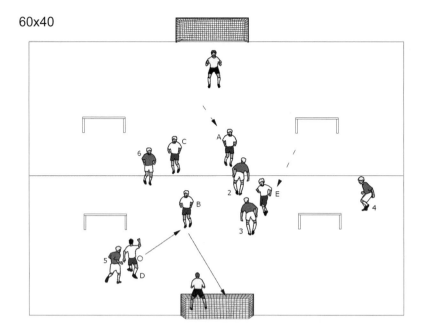

1. In this situation high pressure play by (D) has won possession close to the opponent's goal, which has resulted in a pass to (B) who was the defensive support at first and is now the attacking support, and (B) has scored a goal from the excellent defending of first (D) as the pressing player and the team as a whole, giving (5) no good options to pass to.

2. (E) and (A) both pushed onto opponents to help (D) and (B) and the full team pressure helped (D) win the ball.

3. **Coaching Points for Defending:**
   a) Quick pressure on the ball by the first defender
   b) Close Support by the 2nd defender
   c) Full team pressure closing the spaces down around and close to the ball
   d) Winning possession

CROSSING & FINISHING GAMES

70x50

COMPOSURE
ZONES
5 yds wide

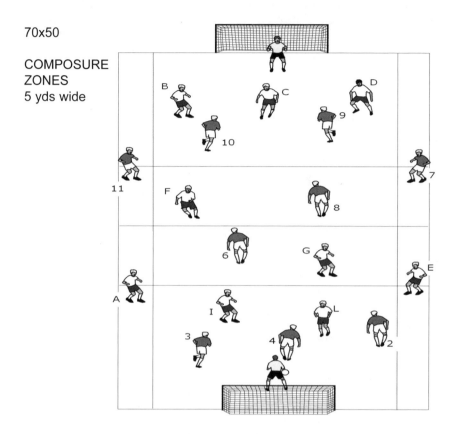

GAME OBJECTIVE: IMPROVING CROSSING AND
FINISHING TECHNIQUES

Working both ways this is a quick transition play session using wide players as the focal points to ensure lots of crosses. You can overload areas: for instance, if your players are particularly poor in finishing have only one defender against two attackers. You can determine any strategy you like and tailor the session to the number of players you have to work with. Wide players perform in channels and no defenders can encroach into these zones, ensuring a constant supply of crosses both ways. The field is short and tight to make sure lots of crossing and finishing takes place at both ends of the field.

COACHING POINTS IN CROSSING AND FINISHING

1. **Head Up** – Glance from the crosser, to see where the players are (attackers, defenders, the keeper).Sometimes the crosser doesn't have time to do this, he just gets the ball into the danger area and expects players to be there.

2. **Decision** – When,Where and How to cross. As early as possible to give defenders as little time as possible to position themselves.

3. **Technique of the Cross** –
   a) A good first touch out of your feet to set the cross up but looking also to where the ball is going and where the attackers are to receive the cross.
   b) Balanced position with the non kicking foot alongside the ball pointing in the direction you want the cross to go. Use of techniques to produce the type of delivery (below), kicking through the ball with correct timing.

4. **Types of Cross** – They can include:
   a) Crosses that are driven low with power (usually to the near post).
   b) Swerved crosses. For example, around a defender using the body position as a guide (near or far post).
   c) Chipped crosses from the goal line (usually to the far post).
   d) Longer, higher trajectory crosses to the far post and past it (to opposite wide player who can shoot at goal or head or pass it back into the danger zone).
   e) Pull back crosses or passes to a midfield player coming in late.

5. **Runs of the Players** – Near post / Far post, away from the ball initially to come back if possible (to lose markers). When a striker runs away from the ball the defender has the problem that when he looks at the ball, he can't see the player he is marking or that player's movement; when he looks at the player, he can't see the delivery of the ball.

6. **Timing of the Run** – As Late as possible and as Fast as possible (so you are difficult to mark plus you don't get into the correct position too early).The player making the near post run must use the post as a guide. If he runs past the near post to receive then it will be difficult to get a shot or header on target.Try to time the run so the ball is arriving as you are arriving, then it's a straight shot or header.

7. **Angle of the Run** – Into the line of the crossed ball, not across it.

8. **The Attacking Finish** – Contact on the ball is probably one touch only using the head or foot. Use the momentum of the crossed ball for power.

1. GAME CONDITIONS

a) Start with the keeper who serves the ball to the wide defenders creating space breaking wide. They must find a wide player with a pass , it can be a player on the same side or a diagonal pass to the other side. Wide player gets a cross in .

b) The ball to midfield players then to wide players.

c) The ball to forwards,then to wide players.

d) To forwards who must link with midfield with a pass who must then pass to wide players.You can mix this up depending on how you want to play.It helps focus the players' minds on where and how to pass and support. Finish with free play and see how they do it for themselves.

e) Teams must stay in their thirds to get an idea of team shape but can work up to the edge of each third of the field.Once a clear shape is established, let it go free and observe movement between the thirds. See if players fill in for one another. For example, if a defender makes a run forward does a midfield player fill in? Where does the defender recover to when that team loses the ball?

f) To ensure that the teams work up and down the field, condition the game so the team in possession can't score unless the defenders of that attacking team are up and over the defending third line.Play offside from this line. This pushes midfield players forward into anticipation area positions closer to goal, thus creating a better chance to regain possession should a defender head the ball clear.

g) Crossers only have two touches to make them concentrate more on their first touch which sets them up for the cross.

h) Have no one stationed in wide areas but when a player goes in there to receive a pass or runs the ball in he is unopposed. Once the cross is made he comes back into the game. This ensures that most players get a chance to get in wide areas to cross. For example a forward makes a run wide and the second forward and wide midfield player become the two forwards to receive the cross.

1. COACHING POINTS

a) Creating Space in wide areas.

b) Decision Making, where, when and how to cross.

c) Quality of Passing.

d) Quality of Crossing.

e) The Runs of Strikers.

f) Support Play of players.

g) Compactness of defenders, condensing play.

h) Quick build up play.

3. INDIVIDUAL AND TEAM WORK

a) Far wide player joins in on the cross for anything that is played beyond the two strikers.

b) Near and Far post runs.

c) Co-ordination of the two strikers and the attacking midfield player.

d) Link up plays between the lines. For example, setting up plays from the keeper to strikers to midfielders to defenders, and how they link up beyond this.

e) Diagonal passing, not just down one side. For example, the wide left defender passing to the wide right attacker (switching play).

f) Use of width in attack, particularly from wide defenders (fullbacks) and wide midfield players to get crosses in.

As you can see, this game can bring in many facets of soccer and you can condition it so you work on one facet at a time (quality of crossing or passing, movement of strikers, pushing out of defenders, link play of midfield, use of width in attack, two touch play etc). The list is endless and is only restricted by your own imagination.

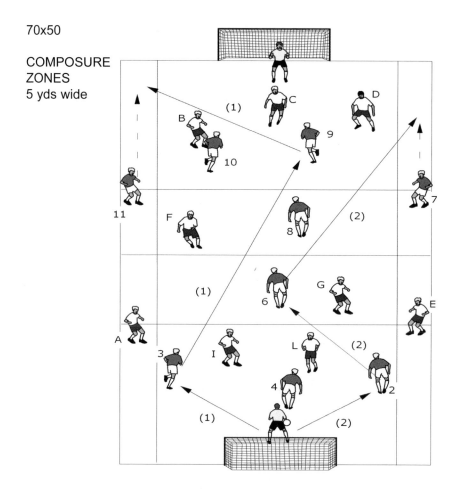

70x50

COMPOSURE
ZONES
5 yds wide

1. Keeper to full back, diagonal pass to a midfielder who passes to a wide player to cross. Keeper to full back to a striker who is closed down and can't turn, so plays the ball wide for a cross. Look at movement of strikers and support players. If the ball is played into a striker who can shoot, he should shoot, even if the ball hasn't gone wide yet. Generally, work the session using width but not to the extent that decisions are made which contradict actual game expectations.

2. **Coaching Points:**
   a) Creating Space
   b) Quality Passing
   c) Using width in attack d) Quality Crossing e) Attitude to Score with one touch in the box

70x50

COMPOSURE
ZONES
5 yds wide

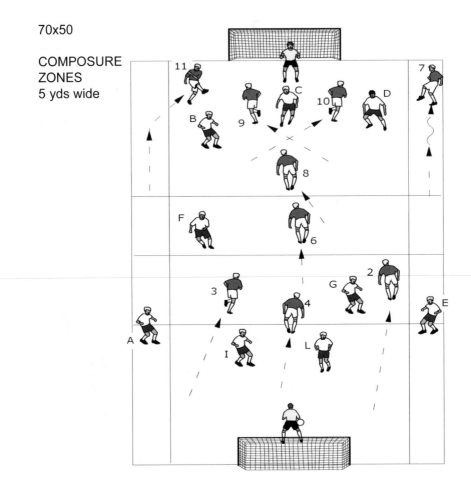

1. Picking one of the choices of attack from the previous slide, this is the finishing set up with players attacking various areas on the field and the whole
   team moving up the field to maintain their compact shape from the back.
   (7)'s cross is early to the near post, behind the retreating defenders.

2. (11) can come inside for the delivery beyond the far post. (9) and (10) may
   attack the opposite posts, depending on their initial movement to get free
   from defenders.

3. We have left the defending teams players in their original positions to
   emphasize the movement of the attacking team. Note that (I) and (L) are left
   offside by the forward movement of the attacking team's defenders.

160

70x50

COMPOSURE
ZONES
5 yds wide

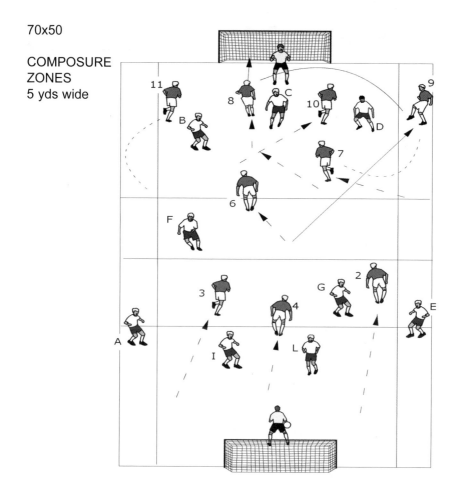

1. An example of a striker (9) moving wide to receive a pass to end up cross-ing the ball. The cross arrives at the far post area for (8) to attack and hope-fully score a goal from the move.

2. Striker (10) becomes the near post area player, Midfielder (8) becomes the player attacking the far post area, (11) attack beyond the far post, the initial passer (6) attacks the central area around or just inside the box, (7) moves into an anticipation area around the box also, and the attacking defensive players (2), (3) and (4) all move up the field along with the keeper, maintain-ing their compactness as a team from the back to the front.

60x40

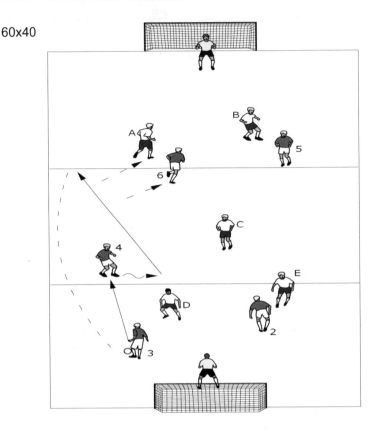

1. In these games the focus is on creating overlapping situations.

2. The overlapping game is a 6 v 6 game and we have an example of a back player (3) working with a midfield player (4) performing an overlap in a wide area of the field.

3. (4) brings the ball inside to clear the space for (3) making the overlapping run. Note also striker (6) moving inside to clear the space in front of (3), taking the defender (A) away also. (3) can now continue the run forward with the ball into space to get into a likely crossing position. If (A) were to stay in the space to try to stop the forward run of (3), then (6) is available to receive a pass inside from (3).

4. Use this game set up to develop any particular combination play, a give and go combination for example.

60x40

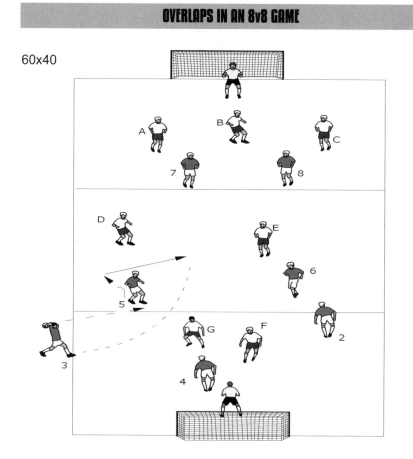

1. Now taking it into an 8 v 8 game. Here is an example of a throw-in situation where the free overlap to begin the game again is shown.

2. You could argue this is an "under-lap" because it is coming inside but it is still technically passing and overlapping the receiver. Of course the "when" and "where" of overlapping is important and this must be emphasized and taught but we just want to get the players performing overlap movements.

3. **Coaching Points:**
    a) Does the player need support behind or in front?
    b) Create Space – Move inside with the ball to open it up outside.
    c) Communication – Support player can call "Hold" to gain time to get into position.
    d) Timing of the run – Go wide (angle and distance).
    e) Player on the ball passes or uses the run as a decoy to come inside and attack.

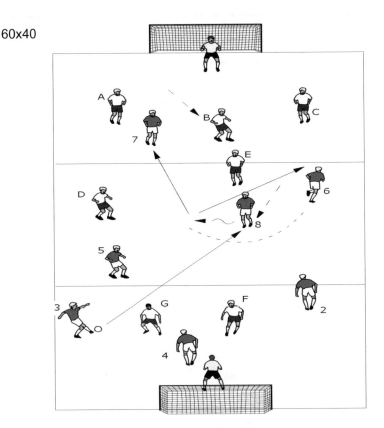

60x40

1. Continuing on with the theme, if a long pass is played forward and the run to overlap is too far for the passer, then the next closest player must perform the overlap.

2. Here (3) plays a good ball forward into the feet of (8) who comes short to receive. (6) makes an overlap run around (8) and we have shown two possible eventualities. (8) can pass to overlapping player (6) or if, for example, (B) is drawn to cover (E) coming inside with the ball and (C) covers the overlapping run of (6) who now acts as a decoy, then (8) can pass to (7) who is in a free position to shoot at goal in this example.

3. The situations created by a simple overlap run are endless but the point is that overlapping runs unsettle defenses and players should be encouraged to make them. They must be aware also that they are making the run not just for themselves but also unselfishly for a teammate to receive the pass instead.

164

60x40

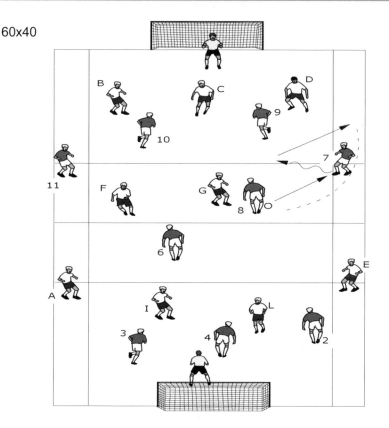

1. Working both ways, this is a quick transition play session using wide players as the focal points to ensure we get lots of overlap plays and crosses in. You can overload areas. For instance, if your players are particularly poor in finishing put only one defender against two attackers and so on. Players have to overlap the wide player when they pass the ball to him and get the cross in unopposed.

2. Wide players perform in channels and no defenders can encroach into these zones, ensuring a constant supply of crosses both ways. Players stay in the attacking half of the field. The field is short and tight to make sure lots of crossing and finishing takes place at both ends.

TWO THEMES IN ONE GAME

70x50

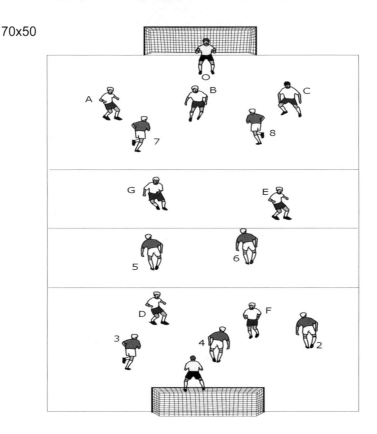

GAME OBJECTIVE: COUNTERING BOTH PRESSING AND ONE TOUCH PLAY

1. We are using an 8 v 8 set up to show the examples of playing a game focusing at various times on winning possession quickly using a high pressing style of play and also playing a quick passing one and two touch game to maintain possession of the ball. Use whatever numbers you have for training, these concepts will work from a small 3 v 3 up to as many players as you like.

2. The principles of each will apply during the three main moments in the game:
    - a) when we have possession,
    - b) when the opponents have possession, and
    - c) when possession changes from one team to another.

70x50

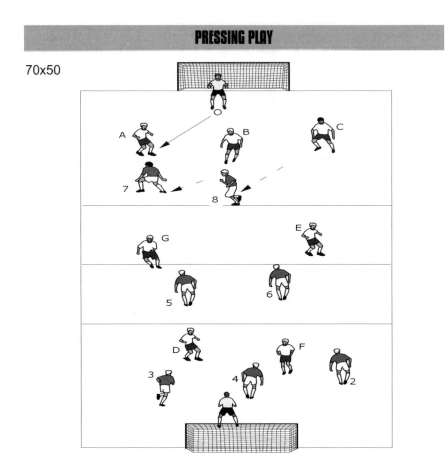

1. This is a high pressure game to encourage the team to try to win the ball as early and as far up the field as possible both as individuals and in the team concept.

2. The main focus is on defending to win the ball to give our team more pos session. Ask the pressing player to call "ball" so everyone knows this player is the one to make the immediate challenge. Have the next closest player, the support player, call "right" or "left" to help the pressing player decide which way to force the ball. All the other players adjust their positions off this combination.

3. To score, the player on the ball just has to get the ball to his own keeper who is in the opposite goal, which means pressure has to be immediate because this player can score from anywhere, even a chip into the keeper's hands is a goal. Or just have an open goal to play into if you have no keepers.

70x50

1. Ask yourself, what does this force the opponents to do?

2. High pressure means the opponent has little time on the ball. So the way to counter high pressure play is to develop one and two touch passing play to prevent the pressing players from getting too close to gain possession with a tackle or forcing a bad pass and giving possession away just through the pressure itself.

3. For the team with the ball, the awareness training we do is designed to teach and develop the quick thinking that this requires: looking before receiving and looking ahead of the game to where the pass will go. This means less time is needed on the ball but it is especially effective if the opponents are applying high pressure. Encourage the team with the ball to play this way to make it more difficult for the pressing to team to be successful.

Coaching Points for One and Two Touch Play:

a) Awareness of teammates' positions, opponents' positions and where space is on the field before receiving a pass.

b) Quality, and especially the "Weight" of the pass to a teammate to allow a one touch pass off if necessary

c) Getting feet into position to receive early

d) Quick decision making

e) Quality and speed of the next pass (one or two touch)

f) Support positions: Movement "off the ball" of teammates to help the player on the ball move it quickly and have immediate options

g) Maintaining possession as a team

Coaching Points for Pressing Play:

a) Quick Pressure by the first defender

b) Support Play by the closest second defender

c) Balanced Covering Play behind by the third defender

d) Team defensive shape

SMALL SIDED GAME DEVELOPMENT

3V3 SMALL SIDED GAMES

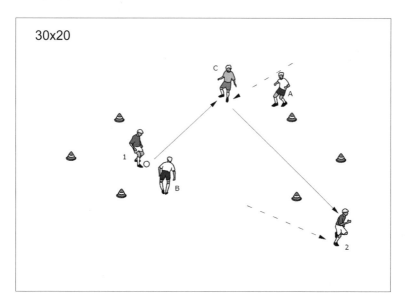

30x20

GAME OBJECTIVE: MAINTAINING POSSESSION IN AN OVERLOAD GAME

1. Try a 2 v 2 + 1 to start. Maybe the coach can be the neutral player to help the players make the session work, especially with younger, less experienced players. Or use a player to be the neutral player.

2. The neutral player plays for whichever team has the ball so is always attacking.

3. This can be used if it is difficult to get a game going with equal numbers on each side and is a perfect overload situation to begin.

4. Maybe restrict the coach to one or two touches as we need the players to be touching and playing with the ball, not the coach, who is there only to help get the game going successfully.

5. Once some success is gained then move on to the 3 v 3 game.

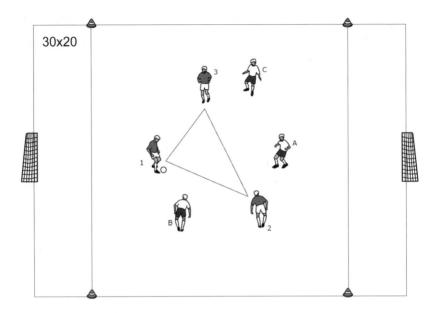

30x20

GAME OBJECTIVE: SSG OFFERING THE OPPORTUNITY OF LOTS OF TOUCHES ON THE BALL FOR ALL THE PLAYERS

1. Mini soccer in three's is a great way for young players to learn how to play the game. Coaches try to teach the game where players support in triangles and in a team of three a natural triangle forms. This is important at ALL age groups, but especially for U8s and U9s.

2. It guarantees lots and lots of touches for each player and in the formative years especially it is vital for the players to work on their technical ability. It provides many opportunities for each player to pass, dribble, shoot, turn and tackle.

3. Only one ball between six players.

4. This is a great medium to start this development but also within a game situation.

5. When a player is on the ball he should always have two pass options.

6. One player can be the goalkeeper and also the last defender and can pick up the ball anywhere within the 5 yard line. You must encourage this player to move up and out of this zone to support his two teammates when they gain possession. Or just play without goalkeepers.

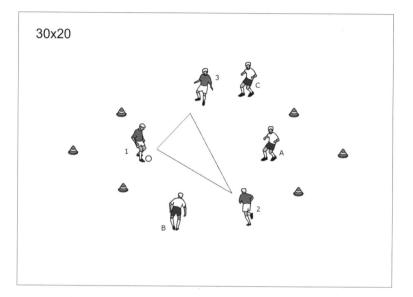

30x20

1. The goals ensure that the ball is in play all the time and that players move off the ball to support. To score a goal through the triangular goals one player has to receive the ball on the other side. No one is allowed inside the triangle.

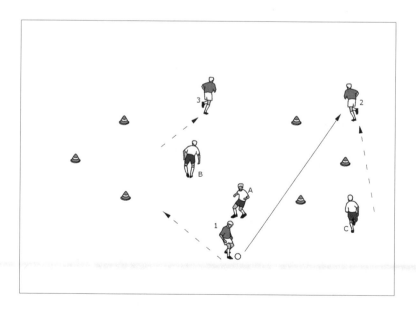

1. **Rules:**
   a) Once a team scores, they have to try to score in the other goal.
   b) If possession changes hands and the ball is regained, the team in possession can attack any goal until they score, then they must attack the other goal.
   c) When they get good, limit to fewer touches on the ball.

2. Here (1) passes through the triangular goal to (2) who has run into space to receive the pass.

3. (3) has moved off the ball into space to receive the pass and attack the other goal. (1) also is on the move to the other goal already.

40x20

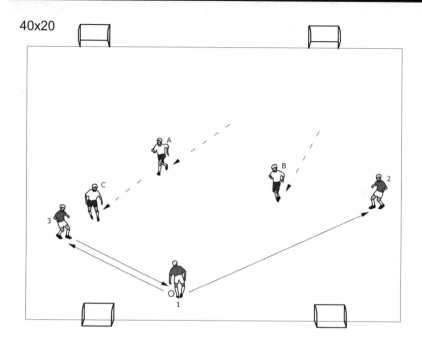

GAME OBJECTIVE: DEVELOPING EFFECTIVE WIDTH IN ATTACK

1. Use two wide positioned goals for each team to attack. This is designed to encourage players to spread out when they attack and to switch play; change direction if one route is blocked.

2. Look for quick transition and movement off the ball to create space, players should attack the space when it is on to do so. The first thought of the player on the ball should still be, "Can I run or pass the ball forward".

3. **Coaching Points:**
   a) Creating Space – for yourself and your teammates.
   b) Decision – When, Where and How to pass the ball.
   c) Technique – The Quality of the pass (Accuracy, Weight, Angle).
   d) Support Positions of teammates (Angle, Distance and Communication). In front and behind.
   e) Switch Play using width in attack, drawing defenders to one side of the field then switching the play quickly to attack the other open side to score. Here the ball is played to (3) from (1), the defending team is drawn towards defending their right side goal. The attacking team stays spread out and this situation shows how a pass back to (1) then quickly across to (2) can open up an attack to the other left side goal or even a direct pass to (2).

179

E): A 3 v 3 "WITH INSIDE FIELD GOALS PASSING, SUPPORT AND COMBINATION PLAY" SMALL SIDED GAME

40x20

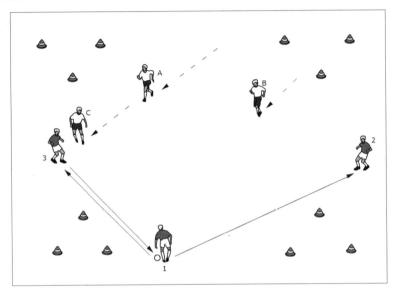

GAME OBJECTIVE: DEVELOPING EFFECTIVE WIDTH IN ATTACK AND MAINTAINING POSSESSION

1. Use two wide positioned goals for each team to attack.This is designed to encourage players to spread out when they attack and to switch play; change direction if one route is blocked.

2. Look for quick transition and movement off the ball to create space but attack the space when it is on to do.

3. **Coaching Points:**
    a) Creating Space – for yourself and your teammates.
    b) Decision – When, Where and How to pass the ball.
    c) Technique – The Quality of the pass (Accuracy, Weight, Angle).
    d) Support Positions of teammates (Angle, Distance and Communication). In front and behind.
    e) Switching Play using width in attack, drawing defenders to one side of the field then switching the play quickly to attack the other open side to score. Here the ball is played to (3) from (1), the defending team is drawn towards defending their right side goal. The attacking team stays spread out and this situation shows how a pass back to (1) then quickly across to (2) can open up an attack to the other left side goal or even a direct pass to (2).

180

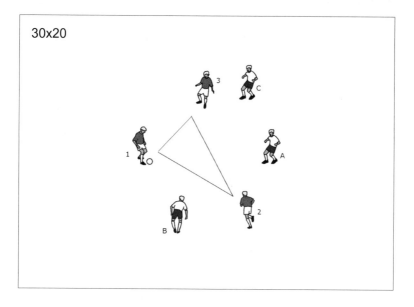

30x20

GAME OBJECTIVE: DEVELOPING DRIBBLING SKILLS

1. A small sided game where the players can only score by dribbling the ball to the end line and stopping it there.

2. This is designed to increase the likelihood of players dribbling with the ball.

3. Looking to create lots of 1 v 1 situations on the field of play.

4. **Coaching Points:**
   a) 1 v 1 Dribbling Play encouraged
   b) When and where to dribble (Safety and Risk areas)
   c) Positive attitude to dribbling
   d) Support positions to create 1 v 1 opportunities (spreading out)
      No goals are used.

5. To score, a player must dribble the ball under control over the goal line. Look to encourage 1 v 1's, work on improving ball control with quick movement. Decision making to improve when and where to dribble.

6. This practice can be applied with the same principles with larger numbers of players such as 6 v 6 etc.

1. Here attacker (3) beats defender (C) and runs the ball forward and stops it on the line. For younger players who may have more difficulty stopping the ball, have a designated area at both ends of the field for them to run the ball in so they have an area of about 5 yards to stop the ball in.

2. **Coaching Points:**
    a) Creating Space – For yourself to receive the ball.
    b) Decision – When and where to dribble (less likely in the defending third, most likely in the attacking third).
    c) Technique –Tight Close Control on receiving the ball, use of body to dummy an opponent, ability to change pace and direction, established dribbling skills, a positive attitude to beat the player.
    d) Runs of Teammates – To support or to take opponents away to leave a 1 v 1 situation
    e) End Product – beating an opponent in a 1 v 1 situation.

3. We are encouraging players to make quick observations and quick decisions often resulting in a player passing the ball early to avoid being caught in possession, but this game also helps players who are good at dribbling by enabling them to identify situations in advance to allow them to get in a good position to take a player on in a 1 v 1 situation. These could include: opening the body up to receive and face up to an opponent, seeing the immediate opponent has no cover on so you can attack 1 v 1, seeing that the defender is early and identifying the best side to attack, seeing you have no support and so must attack 1 v 1 etc.

30x20

GAME OBJECTIVE: IMPROVING RUNNING WITH THE BALL TECHNIQUE

1. Small sided game with the emphasis on running with the ball.

2. To score, the player on the ball has to run the ball into the marked area. Here (1) runs the ball in chased by (C), then must look to pass to another player and attack the opposite way. Once the team has scored they keep possession and can attack the other end zone.

3. **Coaching Points:**
   a) Run with the ball whenever possible
   b) Run with your head up, looking around, not down at the ball
   c) First touch to be forward and out of the feet
   d) Keep the ball moving
   e) If you can't run with the ball, look for a give and go and then run again
   f) Have the positive attitude to run at them to score.

4. Build an overload into the game if necessary with an extra floating player if it is too difficult to get free with equal numbers, making it a 4 v 3 in favor of the attacking team.

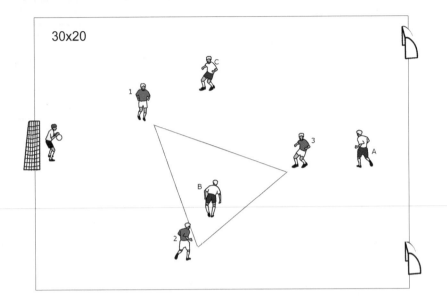

30x20

GAME OBJECTIVE: DEVELOPING TWO THEMES IN ONE GAME; SHOOTING TECHNIQUE AND PASSING AND SUPPORT PLAY

1. Bring in a keeper to play in the big goal and have a 3 v 3 game.

2. One team focuses on shooting and the other on developing passing and support and changing the point of attack.

3. Lots of opportunity to get both themes in with only three players per team.

4. Have both teams take a turn at playing using both themes alternately.

5. As you can see above, natural triangles form on the field between the three players and they learn to move off each other and adjust their positions according to the needs of the game.

6. Organization: Two small goals across from a full size goal. Extra balls kept in the large goal. Field dimensions according to the abilities of the players.

7. Rules: Team defending the large goal gets a goalkeeper. All restarts begin with the goalkeeper. 4+GK attack the two small goals, 4 attack the large goal.

8. High quality possession passing and support. Working on two themes: shooting (the lettered team) and switching the point of the attack (the numbered team).

184

GAME OBJECTIVE: IMPROVING SHOOTING

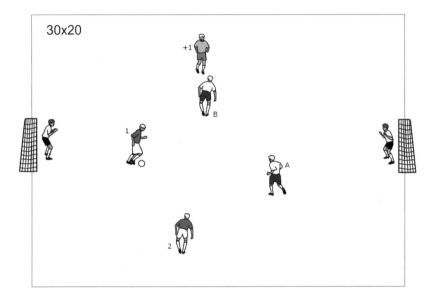

It can be a 2 v 2 plus 1 with keepers or a 3 v 3 with keepers.

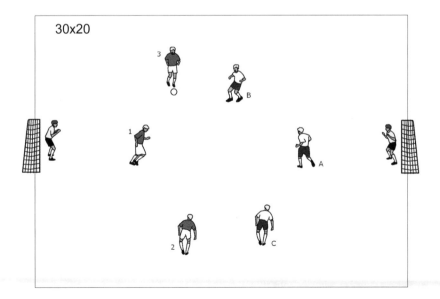

1. Two large goals to encourage success. Shorter field so lots of shots on goal because players are nearly always in shooting positions.Initially have the two team / two ball set up so there is no opposition, enabling players working both ways to get lots of shots in.Once a team has worked a position to shoot and has taken the shot, that team's keeper sets up another attack.

2. Progress it to the competitive even sided game.

3. **Coaching Points:**
    a) Quick shooting.
    b) Rebounds.
    c) Transitions.
    d) Quick break counter attack
    e) Quick Short Passing
    f) Quick defending and pressuring
    g) Goalkeeping practice

4. Players must be particularly aware of where teammates are,where the opposing players are, and the keeper's position, because the space to work in is small and the time they have on the ball is short.

5. Hence development of the mental side of the game, seeing situations quickly and acting upon them, is very important to the player to help him have success in scoring goals. The less time the players have to make the correct decisions to be successful, the more important it is to train them to be able to cope with these pressure situations.

SMALL SIDED GAME DEVELOPMENT

4V4 SMALL SIDED GAMES

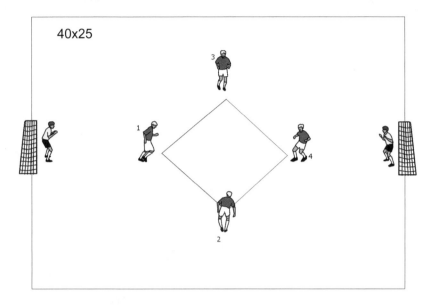

40x25

GAME OBJECTIVE: DEVELOPING ATTACKING AND DEFENDING TEAM PLAY

1. There are no set positions but there is a positional theme to work from which is the diamond. All previous game set ups can be applied in the 4 v 4 game.

2. **Coaching Points:**
   a) Correct Positioning when attacking and Defending.
   b) Maintaining Possession and dictating the direction of play by running with the ball, passing and dribbling.
   c) Forward passing where possible but if not then positioning for back or sideway passing.
   d) Movement as a team forward, backward, sideways left and right.
   e) Communication – verbal and non verbal (body language).

4. **Techniques involved:** Passing, receiving and turning, controlling the ball, dribbling, shielding and shooting. Defending.

5. All the above work requires anticipation and being able to read situations in advance. Field dimensions are generally 40 x 20 yds but can be changed according to the ages and abilities of the players involved

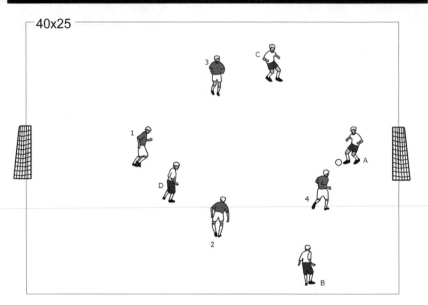

40x25

GAME OBJECTIVE: TEACHING INDIVIDUAL AND TEAM DEFENDING

1. The main idea here is for the defending team to condense the area the ball can be played into,the defending team becomes a diamond within the opponent's attacking diamond. (4) forces (A) one way and the rest of the team adjusts their positions off this. (3) protects the space inside but can close down (C) if the ball is passed, (2) and (1) are in the same situation and this results in the diamond being shorter and tighter. As the opponents move, the defending team must move to compensate. Also, if any pass is played behind (1), (2) or (3), they should be first to the ball.

2. **Coaching Points:**
    a) Pressure – 1 v 1 defending to win the ball, delay or force a bad pass.
    b) Support – position of immediate teammate (angle, distance and communication).
    c) Cover – positions of teammates beyond the supporting player.
    d) Recovering and Tracking should the ball go past our position, recovery run to goal side of the ball and tracking the run of a player.
    e) Regaining Possession and creating Compactness from the back (pushing up as a unit).

3. The objectives of defending are to disrupt the other team's build up, make play predictable, prevent forward passes and ultimately regain possession of the ball. Techniques include – pressuring, marking, tackling and winning the ball.

TWO THEMES IN ONE GAME

C): A 4 v 4 "SHOOTING AND DRIBBLING" DOUBLE THEMED SSG GAME OBJECTIVES: DEVELOPING TWO THEMES IN ONE GAME

40x25

D): A 4 v 4 "SWITCHING THE POINT OF ATTACK AND DRIBBLING" DOUBLE THEMED SMALL SIDED GAME

40x25

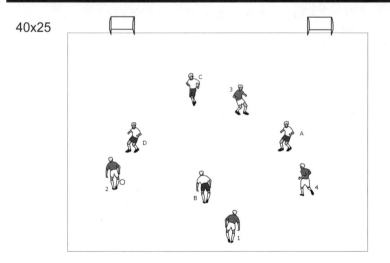

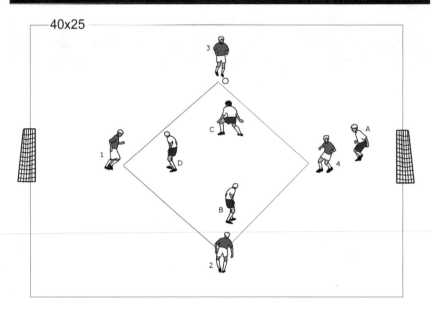

40x25

GAME OBJECTIVES: SMALL SIDED GAMES ENCOURAGING LOTS OF TOUCHES ON THE BALL FOR EACH PLAYER AND DEVELOPING ATTACKING AND DEFENDING AS INDIVIDUALS AND AS A TEAM

1. Can also be 3 v 3 (or 5 v 5). Players referee their own games. Each game lasts 4 minutes (you can vary this time).

2. **Structure:** Each player receives a number that they keep for all the games.

3. **Scoring System:** Each player on the team receives a point for every goal his team scores in a particular game – up to a maximum of 3 points.

4. Each person on the team receives the following, for a win: 3 points, a draw: 1 point, a defeat: 0 points.

5. **Example:** 1, 4 ,7 score 2 goals v 10, 2, 5 who score 3 goals therefore: 1, 4, 7 receive 2 points (for two goals, nothing for the defeat so score total of 2 points each player for the game).
10, 2, 5 receive 6 points (for 3 goals, plus 3 points for the win for total of 6 points each player for the game).
Therefore a player can score a maximum of 6 points in any one game.

6. Play a number of games rotating the players each game and add up all the points for each player at the end of the contest.

SMALL SIDED GAME DEVELOPMENT

6V6 SMALL SIDED GAMES

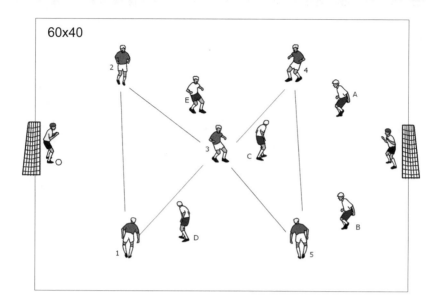

60x40

GAME OBJECTIVE: TEACHING ATTACKING AND DEFENSIVE TEAM PLAY

1. The basic shape is a double triangle, again a positional theme where players are encouraged to interchange then return to a basic shape when the time is right. You could use a 2 – 2 – 1 formation also to allow a 2 v 1 over load at the defensive end.

2. **Coaching Points:**
   a) Create Space - players spread out to be in position to receive the ball.
   b) Decision – when, where and how to pass.
   c) Technique – Quality of the pass (Accuracy, weight and angle).
   d) Support Positions of teammates (angle, distance, communication).
   e) End Product – shots on goal. Rebounds.
   f) The themes you can concentrate on one at a time include, Creating Space as a team, Forward passes to Feet and Space, Switching Play as a team, Running with the Ball, One and Two Touch Play, Passing and Support Play, Diagonal Runs without the Ball (diagonal runs, Overlaps, blindside runs, under laps), Forward diagonal Runs to Receive, Receiving and Turning, When and Where to Dribble.

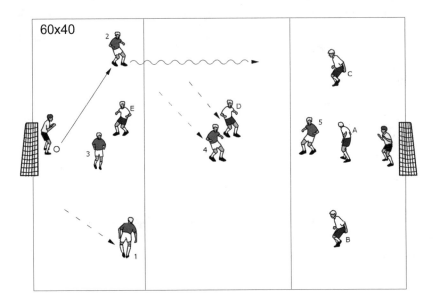

GAME OBJECTIVE: IMPROVING RUNNING WITH THE BALL TECHNIQUE

1. Here the theme is running with the ball, particularly from the back. Use the progressions to get it going.

2. **Coaching Points :**
   a) Creating Space – Players breaking wide to receive the ball from the keeper.
   b) Decision – Can I run with the ball or should I pass?
   c) Technique – Key factors of running with the ball: head up, good first touch out of your feet, run in a straight line (the shortest route forward) with pace, use your front foot to control the ball.
   d) Quality of Pass / Cross / Shot / Dribble at the end of the run.
   e) Support Positions – support in front, fill in behind.

3. When you get to 6 v 6 it may be useful to change the shape of the teams to 3 – 1 – 1 from a 2 – 1 – 2 so there is a 3 v 1 overload at the back to help players run out with the ball. The space is usually in the wide areas for this movement. This allows for a greater chance of success in the practice until players are comfortable and confident performing the theme.

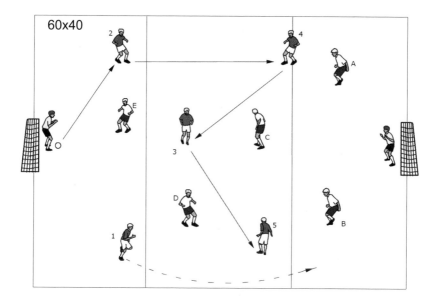

GAME OBJECTIVE: TEACHING WHEN AND WHERE TO CHANGE THE FIELD

1. **Coaching Points :**
   a) Creating Space as individuals and a team.
   b) Decision – When, where and how to pass the ball.
   c) Technique – Quality of the pass, can I pass it forward or should I switch the play?.
   d) Support Positions – To switch the play (open stance to receive and pass).
   e) Switching the Play – From one side of the field to the other.

2. In the above example the team has attacked down one side of the field but has been stopped from further progress by good defending, so they come back and switch the play to the other side.

3. A great run by (1) on the overlap complements this move making a 2 v 1 situation on the opposite side of the field from which they started the move.

60x40

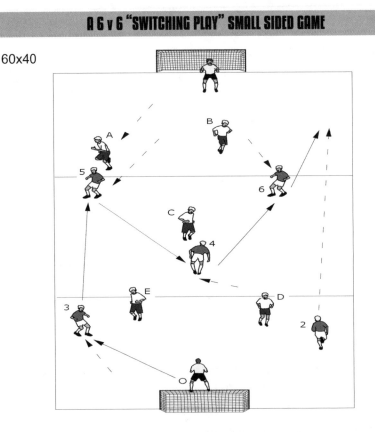

GAME OBJECTIVE: TEACHING WHEN AND WHERE TO CHANGE THE FIELD

1. **Coaching Points :**
   a) Creating Space as individuals and a team.
   b) Decision – When, where and how to pass the ball.
   c) Technique – Quality of the pass, can I pass it forward or should I switch the play?
   d) Support Positions – To switch the play (open stance to receive and pass).
   e) Switching the Play – From one side of the field to the other.

2. In the above example the team has attacked down one side of the field but has been stopped from further progress by good defending so they come back and switch the play to the other side. A great run by (2) on the overlap complements this move, making a 2 v 1 situation on the opposite side of the field from which they started.

3. Here is a final example of the importance of switching the attack and movement off the ball to help this happen: (6) could pass to (2) to cross the ball in for (5) who can make a run back into the target zone.

D): A 6 v 6 "CREATING SPACE" SMALL SIDED GAME

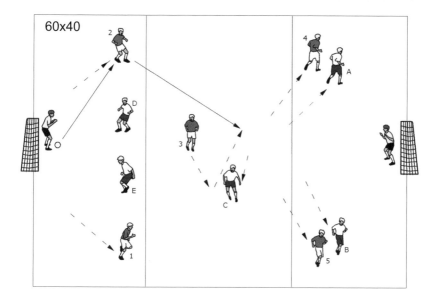

60x40

GAME OBJECTIVE: CREATING SPACE AS A TEAM

1. Here the players work to get free of their markers with movement off the ball. They create space for themselves and / or for their teammates.

2. **Coaching Points:**
    a) Creating Space – Spreading out as a team.
    b) Decision – When, where and how to Create Space.
    c) Technique – passing and receiving.
    d) Support Positions of players; angles and distances, movement off the ball.

3. In the above example, (1) and (2) break wide to create space and offer two options for the keeper. (2) receives the pass and (3) runs off (C) to check back to receive the pass in space. (4) and (5) create space in front of the receiving player by making split runs to move (A) and (B) away from where (3) wants to attack and shoot at goal.

4. If either (A) or (B) fail to track the two strikers and instead stay in the space in front to defend against (3), then (3) can pass to whichever player is left free.

60x40

GAME OBJECTIVE: DEVELOPING DRIBBLING SKILLS IN A TEAM ENVIRONMENT

1. Looking to create 1 v 1 situations in the middle and especially the attacking thirds of the field, focusing on players with a good dribbling technique.

2. **Coaching Points:**
    a) Creating Space – Run the player off to check back and receive to feet.Body position is half turned with the back to the touchline.Where the defender marks determines whether the attacker goes inside or outside.
    b) Attitude to Dribble – Aggressive / Positive.
    c) Decision – Does the attacker run, pass, cross, shoot or dribble?
    d) Technique of Dribbling - when it is on to dribble.How to dribble using moves.
    e) Safety and Risk Areas of the Field – where is it on to dribble?
    f) Runs of the players – to support or create space.

3. Here (5) runs off (B) to create space behind to come back and receive the ball to feet. (5) must shape up with his back to the touchline to be able to see the whole field and all the options available. If (B) doesn't follow, (5) can get the pass in front to attack the goal using (4) to create a 2 v 1 position.

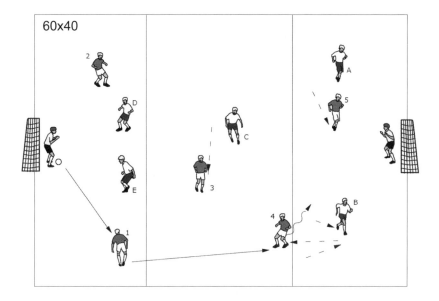

GAME OBJECTIVE: IMPROVING RECEIVING AND TURNING

1. Here the theme is receiving and turning, particularly in the middle and attacking thirds.

2. **Coaching Points:**
   a) Creating Space with movement off the defenders.
   b) Decision – When and where to receive and turn.
   c) Technique – How to receive and turn. The best way, if you have time, is to run your marker off and return to the space you have created for yourself with that movement.
   d) Quality of the Pass into the receiver for ease of control.
   e) Positions of Support of teammates in front and behind the player on the ball.

3. In the above example, (4) runs the defender (B) off away from the ball to check back to receive the pass. (3) positions to support behind as can (1) also but if (4) has turned, (5) makes a run into a receiving position of support in front of the ball to take a shot or create a 2 v 1 situation with (4) by losing the marking of (A). If (4) is a very good dribbler then (5) can run off (A) away from the space in front of goal to leave (4) in a 1 v 1 situation.

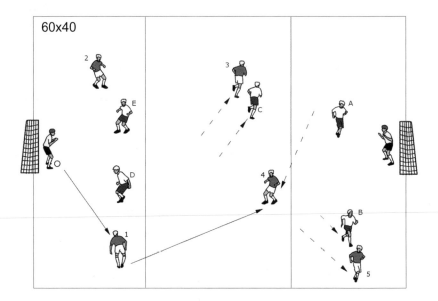

60x40

GAME OBJECTIVE: TEACHING DIAGONAL RUNS "OFF" THE BALL TO CREATE SPACE FOR OTHERS

1. The theme is making diagonal runs with or without the ball to receive or create space for a teammate.When it is a forward diagonal run, the player making it must avoid running offside in a game situation.

2. **Coaching Points:**
   a) Creating Space.
   b) Decision –when and where to pass into the receiver.
   c) Technique – Quality of the pass, particularly the weight, accuracy and timing.
   d) Angle and Timing of the Diagonal Runs, both to create space and to receive the ball.
   e) Support Positions of the players.

3. In the above example, (1) is on the ball to pass it forward. (5) makes a diag onal run away from the center, taking (B) with him. (3) also makes a diago- nally opposite run away from the central area, taking (C) away also.This leaves space for (4) to come short with another diagonal run to receive the pass. (4) may have run (A) off to check back if time was available to do so, thus creating more time and space on the ball. Another way to create space for (4) coming short to receive would be for (5) to make a run towards (4) and cut across the path of (4)'s marker (A) to hold up his run.

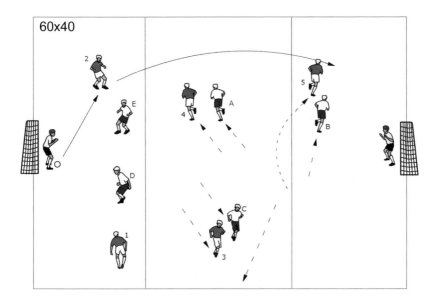

GAME OBJECTIVE: FOCUSING ON DIAGONAL RUNS
TO RECEIVE THE PASS

1. Here (4) goes short, taking (A) with him.

2. This creates space behind (A) for (5) to run into to receive the pass. (3) again runs off (C) to help clear the space.

3. On the next diagram the strikers make opposite diagonal runs to get mid-fielder (3) in centrally.

Another example

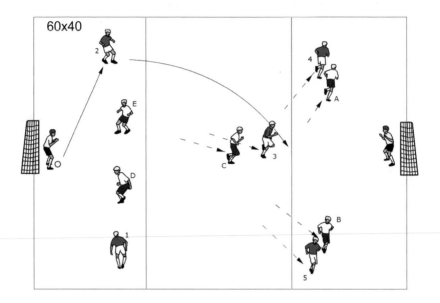

60x40

Coaching Points:
a) Creating Space: Movement off the ball
b) Decision: when and where to pass
c) Technique: Quality of Pass
d) Timing of forward run to receive
e) Support positions of teammates to continue the attack

CONCLUSION

This book is designed to help coaches develop themes in soccer training primarily through game orientated situations.

Some games have a build up to them and natural progressions built in, due to the very nature of the particular theme I feel these plans needed more information.

This applies to several plans, including the Awareness Numbers game (Plan1) has many facets to it that need to be developed, as does the Movement off the Ball (Plan 6), Circle Overload Possession Games (Plan 8), Quick Shooting and Finishing game (Plan 14), and Transitions Through the Thirds (Plan 29) amongst others.

The way the games are set up allows coaches to create easy ways of building into the themed games if they need to.

Players like to play in game focused situations in training and these themed plans should satisfy these needs.

Within the games the coach can stop the session and analyze the theme they are trying to teach through the training situation, and address problems easily. The set up of the games also helps players practice the themes even without too much coaching. Once the coach has explained the set up, the theme comes through clearly through just playing at each stage of progression.

The author hopes you enjoyed the book and any feedback on it that can help to improve the games in any way is welcome.

Please contact him at *wharrison@integraonline.com*

Other Titles Available by Wayne Harrison

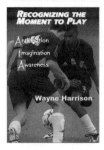

RECOGNIZING THE MOMENT TO PLAY

This unique coaching program focuses on the development of each player's soccer instincts (Anticipation, Imagination, Awareness) through the use of specially designed training sessions. While this is quite possibly the most imortant aspect of a player's soccer development, it is also the most difficult to coach. In this book, the author provides several practical exercises and small sided games to help players *Recognize the Moment to Play*.
Recommended by the English FA
Item#796 - $14.95

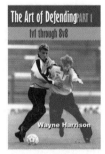

THE ART OF DEFENDING
Part One: 1v1 through 8v8

The art of good defending takes a disciplined mind and body and all players should be taught how to do it properly. This book takes you progressively through the techniques and tactics of defending from 1v1 through to 8v8 small sided situations. This is a very comprehensive and useful book on defense training.

Item#252 - $14.95

THE ART OF DEFENDING
Part Two: Phase Play and 11v11

This second part of Harrison's excellent team defending series covers all aspects of 11v11 defending.
Through phase plays, full squad exercises in which the defense is coached specifically, duties and responsibilities are taught in each third of the field. Well organized and very useful, this book is a must for coaches who need to work on the defensive side of the game.

Item#253 - $14.95

For a full catalog of these and other great soccer titles visit www.reedswain.com or call 800-331-5191